ROYAL
daughters
with
PRIESTHOOD
POWER

{ 7 WAYS LATTER-DAY SAINT
WOMEN RECEIVE *and*
EXERCISE THE PRIESTHOOD }

C. ROBERT LINE

CFI
An imprint of Cedar Fort, Inc.
Springville, Utah

This is not an official publication of The Church of Jesus Christ of Latter-day Saints. The opinions and views expressed herein belong solely to the author and do not necessarily represent the opinions or views of Cedar Fort, Inc. Permission for the use of sources, graphics, and photos is also solely the responsibility of the author.

ISBN 13: 978-1-4621-3581-3

Published by CFI, an imprint of Cedar Fort, Inc.
2373 W. 700 S., Springville, UT, 84663
Distributed by Cedar Fort, Inc., www.cedarfort.com

Library of Congress Control Number: 2019947306

Cover design by Shawnda T. Craig
Cover design © 2019 Cedar Fort, Inc.

Printed in the United States of America

10 9 8 7 6 5 4 3 2 1

Printed on acid-free paper

For my wife, daughters, daughter-in-law,
sisters, mother, and mother-in-law . . .
. . . angels all.

Also by

C. Robert Line

Understanding the Doctrine of God's Time

*Pure Before Thee: Becoming Cleansed and
Changed by Christ*

Parables of Redemption

*Endowed with Power: How Temple Symbols Guide
Us to Christ's Atonement*

Contents

Author's Note

Although the central theme of this book is women and the priest-hood, as stated in the title and subtitle, there will be an exploration of other important related principles. In part one, we will examine the central issue of LDS women and their relationship to the priesthood as declared and defined by scriptures and latter-day prophets and apostles. In part two, we will examine the principle and doctrine of equality, gender roles, and finding balance in life through divinely appointed priorities and perspectives. In part three, we will conclude with an examination of women and the temple experience as it relates to the priesthood. Symbolic temple teachings and views will be explored that can help with a greater understanding of and appreciation for the sacred work that women perform via the priesthood in the house of the Lord. Through the vital principles of womanhood, motherhood, and priesthood, the Lord not only shows his love and concern for women but also prepares them for the eternities.

The Church of Jesus Christ of Latter-day Saints is more committed than any religious institution I know of to the dignity and standing and worth and merit and glory of a woman . . . Now we need to do better, everybody needs to do better, I think society needs to do better, this Church probably needs to do better . . . I think we all need to do better to make sure that that dignity comes through, to make sure that that kind of communication is conveyed . . . we just need to do better to be able to convey that . . . to make sure that everyone understands, including the women of the Church, which I don't think we have done well enough yet.

—Elder Jeffrey R. Holland
Q and A at Harvard University, March 20, 2012

Part 1

WOMEN AND THE PRIESTHOOD

Chapter 1

Perspectives on Women
and the Priesthood

*M*any years ago, I had an intriguing talk with my mother about certain gospel principles. It was just after my appointment as an institute director in the Midwest. The move took our family from Utah to a locale just three hours' drive from where she was living. As we got together for our visit, we quickly delved into myriad questions that had recently troubled her. I answered the best I could as we engaged in a wide range of subjects. Before long, the conversation turned to the priesthood. After discussing a few related issues, my mom made the most intriguing declaration: "I love the Church but just wish I could understand why women are not allowed to have the priesthood." Her statement wasn't intriguing because it was anything new. I had heard such statements before from others, usually in concerned, perplexed, and, at times, even in incensed tones. No, it was intriguing because of *the way* my mother said it. It was so honest, vulnerable, and sincere. Then she inquired of me, "Why are men the only ones who get to have the priesthood?" Her question, like her previous statement, was genuine, heartfelt, and devoid of criticism. Looking back on that day, I must admit that her question, not to mention her candor, caught me off guard. I was at a loss for words, and I probably gave her the "we must take it on faith" answer, or perhaps I proffered some other cultural excuse that revealed my ignorance.

This and other similar experiences have led to me to realize that sometimes we err in understanding, not because the doctrine of Christ is not pure and true, but rather our cultural influences inevitably intertwine with that doctrine, making our understanding of it less clear. I feel the same could be said with an incorrect understanding of the divine role of women and the relationship they have with the priesthood. A recent study found that 70 percent of single women cited "women's issues" as a significant reason they left the Church, and 63 percent of all women cited "women's issues" as a significant reason they left.[1] I recently attended a class where an invited speaker (and gifted instructor, I should add) taught a class where she shared deep, heart-felt feelings regarding these issues, saying that "many women in the Church are in pain. Many women feel marginalized . . . this is a problem within our church culture!" She then shared a personal and somewhat distressing story to illustrate her point. I have asked her permission to share this experience in this book. She consented but asked to remain anonymous.

> I live in what you might call a "powerhouse" ward. We have dozens of BYU professors, returned mission president couples, former stake presidents, bishops, etc. . . . This ward is strong. In Sunday School a few weeks ago, one of my former bishops—a man who I greatly admire— was giving the lesson. He is a man of incredible empathy and kindness, and is one of the most tenderhearted men I have ever met. During the lesson, he spoke of his wife's conversion as a teenager. Although I do not remember the exact words he used, he made the comment that he felt sorry for those missionaries as they were teaching the "worst" kind of investigator/convert. Because, as a missionary, "You don't want to be teaching a teenage girl. You want to baptize someone who would be a future stake president, or someone like that." I sat in stunned silence. I was sitting by two strong and opinionated female BYU professors, who I also think were in shock. Did we really just hear that correctly? Did he really just say there was a hierarchy to the kingdom of God and that the "worst" and least important was a teenage girl? Whether or not that was the message he intended to convey, that is exactly the message I heard. Not a single person in that class—men and women of incredible spiritual strength—spoke up to correct or clarify what he had said. I think that bothered me almost as much as the comment itself. Perhaps we were all still trying to wrap our heads around what we had heard in a kind of "shocked stupor." I don't believe this good man intended to hurt my heart with his words, but he did. And I don't believe that by

1. Mormon Research Foundation, "Understanding Mormon Disbelief." Survey, March 2012.

allowing that kind of comment to stand without correction that we as a class intended to convey our agreement with it. But with our silence, I believe that's exactly what we did.

She went on to say, "I may not be able to change how the world perceives our Church's treatment of women, or how cultural practices in our Church can make women feel inferior, but I can clarify and boldly teach the doctrine Christ taught regarding women. In doing so, I can help [others] separate the doctrine from the culture in our day."[2] I wholeheartedly agree with her assessment and hope to accomplish the same objective in this book. This woman's story and that of my mother are just a few examples that illustrate a dilemma we face in the Church today.

That this difficulty really does exist can further be seen in this statement from President Ballard:

> There are those who question the place of women in God's plan and in the Church. I've been interviewed enough by national and international media to tell you that most journalists with whom I have dealt have had preconceived notions about this topic. Through the years many have asked questions implying that women are second-class citizens in the Church. Nothing could be further from the truth.[3]

Elder Richard G. Scott commented on this dilemma, even taking it a step further: "So many of our sisters are disheartened, even discouraged, and disillusioned." He then said that

> Satan has unleashed a seductive campaign to undermine the sanctity of womanhood, to deceive the daughters of God and divert them from their divine destiny. He well knows women are the compassionate, self-sacrificing, loving power that binds together the human family. He would focus their interests solely on their physical attributes and rob them of their exalting roles as wives and mothers. He has convinced many of the lie that they are third-class citizens in the kingdom of God. That falsehood has led some to trade their divinely given femininity for male coarseness.

---

2. June 2019 Utah Valley Symposium in Orem, Utah. Shared with permission from the presenter.
3. M. Russell Ballard, "Men and Women in the Work of the Lord," devotional address, Brigham Young University, Aug. 20, 2013; emphasis added. See speeches.byu.edu.

One thoughtful Latter-day Saint scholar has concluded,

> I've come to recognize as never before the importance of understanding the priesthood and its associated blessings for women. We're living in a day when equality, power, fairness, and tolerance are touted—often above other virtues. What's more, identity, authority, spirituality, and even God are topics of great confusion for many. Many women, not knowing what blessings they have access to, are not taking full advantage of the spiritual feast available to them. Many men are also confused on the topic.[4]

Over the past twenty-seven years as a religious educator, author, bishop, father, and husband, I have had conversations with many faithful women of the Church on this very topic. These include ward members, students, family members, daughters, relatives, and more. They too have expressed similar concerns, with just as much sincerity and faithfulness as did my mother. I have listened to them, pondered sincerely, prayed humbly, and have poured over inspired writings, both scriptural and prophetic, trying as best as I could to make sense of this sometimes difficult and most important topic. To be fair, my own anecdotal experience suggests that while some LDS women (perhaps many) are not particularly concerned about why women do not hold priesthood authority, many others do consider this a crucial issue.

So why am I writing this book? To be clear, honest, and to the point, I have observed that some important, if not vital, gospel principles are rarely taught or brought up when this topic is discussed, whether in talks, books, lessons, articles, or counseling. To be sure, the scriptures and our prophets have taught the vital points of doctrine discussed in this book. Yet I feel their words and counsel have yet to be assembled in a coherent, unified, and simplified way that will help both women and men truly understand some empowering principles that could, as President Boyd K. Packer has said, help change attitudes and behaviors.

Often when the theme of women and the priesthood is brought up or taught, the focus is usually on related or ancillary topics, which, in my opinion, are put forth as a panacea. While some of these topics are no doubt of vital importance, they often avoid the real issue as to why women

---

4. Barbara Morgan Gardner, "I Have So Much to Learn about the Priesthood," *Ensign*, Mar. 2019.

supposedly do not participate in the priesthood. These topics include but are not limited to

1. Blessings that issue from the priesthood that everyone can receive.
2. The grandeur, importance, and vitality of womanhood and motherhood.
3. The importance of understanding gender role differences in the gospel plan.
4. Sisters have one of the largest and oldest women's organizations in the Relief Society.
5. The special place that women have in God's plan and heart.

The list goes on. Now, all of these are real, true, and wonderful concepts, but they are lacking in that they do not fully address the fact that Latter-day Saint women (and here is the point) do indeed participate in the priesthood, are given priesthood authority, and function with priesthood authority. Furthermore, they exercise priesthood authority and have in mortality (and can have in eternity) the power and authority of the holy priesthood. Each of the foregoing declarations will be explored fully and documented thoroughly in this book.

Women in the Church of Jesus Christ do indeed participate in the priesthood, are given priesthood authority, function with priesthood authority, exercise priesthood authority, and have in mortality and will have in eternity the power and authority of the holy priesthood.

This is not a stretching of the doctrine or a wresting of the scriptures. It's not bending to social pressures that somehow force us to devise an acceptable narrative. Elder Dale G. Renlund recently taught that "women in the Church *frequently exercise priesthood power and authority*, though they are not ordained to priesthood offices."[5]

Furthermore, these doctrines and principles, as we shall see in the coming chapters, have always existed. Let me give a brief analogy using another doctrine. Over a lifelong study of the restored gospel, I have seen a wonderful, deliberate, and even miraculous focus on the doctrine of the grace and mercy of Jesus Christ and His saving powers. Gifted scholars, diligent teachers, and inspired leaders have led the charge to the doctrinal high ground and blessings of Jesus Christ's infinite Atonement through books, articles, songs, and even stage productions. Given the times we live in, this emphasis has been timely and needed. However, no serious student of the gospel would ever conclude that this doctrinal direction and renaissance of grace has been fabricated out of thin air. No, the scriptures that undergird the doctrine of salvation through grace have always been there, particularly and especially in the Book of Mormon. Perhaps we should say that we are now, with the aid of inspired prophets and apostles, getting a better and more complete view of what these scriptures have always meant. Thus, the Lord sees fit in His infinite wisdom to reveal, "line upon line" many great and important things pertaining to the kingdom of God.

One more doctrinal analogy is worth mentioning. In 1978, another needful and inspired doctrinal emphasis came about when the Church announced the revelation that came to President Spencer W. Kimball that "removed all restrictions with regard to race that once applied to the priesthood" (Official Declaration—2). Not long after this wonderful announcement, Elder Bruce R. McConkie gave a talk entitled, "All Are Alike unto God." These are some of his relevant words as they apply to our discussion at hand:

> I would like to say something about the new revelation relative to the priesthood going to those of all nations and races. "He [meaning Christ, who is the Lord God] inviteth them all to come unto him and partake of his goodness; and he denieth none that come unto him,

5. Dale G. Renlund and Ruth L. Renlund, *The Melchizedek Priesthood* (Salt Lake City: Deseret Book, 2018), 18–20; emphasis added.

black and white, bond and free, male and female; and he remembereth the heathen; and all are alike unto God, both Jew and Gentile" (2 Nephi 26:33). These words have now taken on a new meaning. We have caught a new vision of their true significance. This also applies to a great number of other passages in the revelations. Since the Lord gave this revelation on the priesthood, *our understanding of many passages has expanded. Many of us never imagined or supposed that they had the extensive and broad meaning that they do have.* . . . There are statements in our literature by the early Brethren that we have interpreted to mean that [certain people] would not receive the priesthood in mortality. I have said the same things, and people write me letters and say, "You said such and such, and how is it now that we do such and such?" And all I can say to that is that it is time disbelieving people repented and got in line and believed in a living, modern prophet. Forget everything that I have said, or . . . whomsoever has said in days past that is contrary to the present revelation. *We spoke with a limited understanding and without the light and knowledge that now has come into the world.* We get our truth and our light line upon line and precept upon precept. We have now had added a new flood of intelligence and light on this particular subject, and it erases all the darkness and all the views and all the thoughts of the past. They don't matter anymore. It doesn't make a particle of difference what anybody ever said about the . . . matter before the first day of June of this year, 1978. *It is a new day and a new arrangement, and the Lord has now given the revelation that sheds light out into the world on this subject.*[6]

Elder McConkie's reference to the scripture in 2 Nephi 26:33 is intriguing. This scripture was always there in the Book of Mormon, but, as Elder McConkie says,

> These words have now *taken on a new meaning.* We have caught *a new vision of their true significance.* This also applies to a great number of other passages in the revelations. Since the Lord gave this revelation on the priesthood, *our understanding of many passages has expanded.* Many of us never imagined or supposed that they had the *extensive and broad meaning* that they do have.[7]

---

6. Bruce R. McConkie, "All Are Alike unto God," CES Religious Educator's Symposium, Aug. 18, 1978; emphasis added. See speeches.byu.edu.

7. McConkie, "All Are Alike unto God."

In recent years, the Church has further clarified and elaborated on Elder McConkie's sentiments and realizations. In the Church's official gospel topic essay entitled, "Race and Priesthood," the following declaration is given:

> Today, the Church disavows the theories advanced in the past that black skin is a sign of divine disfavor or curse, or that it reflects unrighteous actions in a premortal life; that mixed-race marriages are a sin; or that blacks or people of any other race or ethnicity are inferior in any way to anyone else. Church leaders today unequivocally condemn all racism, past and present, in any form.[8]

I rejoice, as do many members of this Church, in these inspired changes that have come about with respect to priesthood; however, care should be taken not to construe these modifications as changes in doctrine. "Doctrines are eternal and do not change; however, the Lord, through His prophet, may change practices and programs, according to the needs of the people."[9]

I have often wondered if the changes that have occurred have less to do with the Lord's time and more to do with ours. We might ask ourselves, "Are we ready to accept the Lord's will? Are we ready to treat all his children—black and white, bond and free, male and female—with the same respect and love that he does? Could it be that some of these inequalities have more to do with man's history and failings and less to do with God's eternal love for all? Is He waiting for us to want to change, rather than us waiting for him to make the change?"

The point is this: what will be said in this book in regard to women and the priesthood is nothing new. The scriptures in the previous two analogies, the scriptures that will be cited herein, and the inspired statements from Church leaders in the past have always been there. This is to say that the doctrine has not changed, although our understanding over time perhaps does, individually and collectively as a church. (See D&C 1:30.) Furthermore, God often gives clarifying revelation to elucidate and more fully explain the doctrine that is taught in the scriptures. Such a pattern has occurred since the inception of the restoration. After being baptized,

---

8. "Race and Priesthood," Gospel Topics Essays (2016); see churchofjesuschrist.org.
9. "The Living Prophet: The President of the Church," *Teachings of the Living Prophets Student Manual* (Salt Lake City: The Church of Jesus Christ of Latter-day Saints, 2010), 14–27.

Joseph Smith related that he and Oliver Cowdery "were filled with the Holy Ghost, and rejoiced." Then Joseph said, "Our minds being now enlightened, *we began to have the scriptures laid open to our understandings, and the true meaning and intention of their more mysterious passages revealed unto us in a manner which we never could attain to previously, nor ever before had thought of"* (Joseph Smith—History 1:73–74; emphasis added).

In summary, this book is simply my attempt to provide a clear and organized way of presenting these wonderful—albeit sometimes unrecognized—gospel truths. No doubt some who read this book will question the principles therein. That is fine. I only ask that the reader carefully examine the scriptures presented, along with the prophetic statements offered, and ponder them sincerely and with an open mind. Perhaps some will feel that current prophetic voices on the topic of women and the priesthood contradict other voices, friends, or trusted teachers they've had in the past. This might be the case, but let us remember this wise counsel from the Church in 2007:

> Not every statement made by a Church leader, past or present, necessarily constitutes doctrine. A single statement made by a single leader on a single occasion often represents a personal, though well-considered, opinion, but is not meant to be officially binding for the whole Church. With divine inspiration, the First Presidency and the Quorum of the Twelve Apostles counsel together to establish doctrine that is consistently proclaimed in official Church publications. This doctrine resides in the four standard works of scripture, official declarations and proclamations, and the Articles of Faith.[10]

Likewise, Elder Uchtdorf said,

> Some struggle with unanswered questions about things that have been done or said in the past. We openly acknowledge that in nearly 200 years of Church history—along with an uninterrupted line of inspired, honorable, and divine events—there have been some things said and done that could cause people to question . . . And, to be perfectly frank, *there have been times when members or leaders in the Church have simply made mistakes.* There may have been things said or done that were not in harmony with our values, principles, or doctrine.[11]

---

10. "Approaching Mormon Doctrine," commentary, May 4, 2007. See newsroom .churchofjesuschrist.org.

11. Dieter F. Uchtdorf, "Come, Join with Us," *Ensign*, Nov. 2013; emphasis added.

One final thought: this book will not necessarily alleviate any frustrations, afflictions, or pain that may have been unfortunately felt by some Church members over the years regarding issues related to this topic. As we have said, mistakes have sometimes been made; doctrines and principles at times have been incorrectly taught or applied; and most of all, imperfect, yet well intentioned members have *acted* in ways which are, unfortunately, at times flat out wrong. Recently, a wise and consecrated woman in my ward shared the following story at a Church meeting. I have asked her for permission to share this to illustrate my point.

Over the years, I think society has improved the equality between men and women, although gaps still remain. However, when I was in junior high and high school in the 80s, I definitely felt and fought to prove myself against many inequalities. I was always happy I was a girl. I didn't want to be a boy, but I wanted to do what the boys got to do. I loved to get the highest score on a math test just to prove to doubters that girls could do math as well as boys. I would never purposely lose a game to a boy just to make him feel better, although many of my friends did.

I don't even remember exactly what happened or who said it, but one particular Sunday when I was sixteen, something was said about boys and the priesthood that made me feel, once again, like women were a rung below men in the church. I lived in Hawaii at the time while my dad was the director of the library at BYU—Hawaii. After church, I walked up to campus, which was close to my house, and found a spot on the side of the rugby field to sit. I poured out my anger, frustration, and hurt to the Lord, although in the end, it was all summed up in the question, "Do you love, need, and value girls as much as you do boys?"

To this day, what occurred after my pleading to the Lord remains one of strongest answers to a prayer that I have ever received. I had no sooner said "amen" when my whole body was filled with overwhelming feelings, not only of love, but of power and value as well. When I finally recovered enough to head back home, I thought to myself, "If He prefers anyone, I'd have to say girls now!"

As the years have passed, I have gone back to that answer many times when faced with questions, chauvinistic comments, and feelings of being inferior. I don't know all the answers, but I do know, without a doubt, that women are equal partners with men in spiritual power, ability, intelligence, and strength as we work to move the work of the Lord forward in these latter days.

The inclusion of this story, and that of my mother's, is not to demean or disparage the Church nor its teachings. I only share to illustrate the fact that these are real issues that affect real people, many of whom love the Lord and honor and respect priesthood leaders. It is simply my hope in writing this book to share some things that I have learned over a lifetime of Church service. I wish to teach and help others see what I have seen—mainly, that while we do not have doctrinal, scriptural, or general Church leadership problems with the issue of women and the priesthood, we do, in my opinion, have some cultural problems. I realize that what I share in this work could be very sensitive, so I plead for patience, faith, and understanding as we begin this venture of discovering what our Father in Heaven has said through inspiration about His royal daughters having and exercising priesthood power. This book is a personal endeavor and is not intended to represent the official teachings of The Church of Jesus Christ of Latter-day Saints.

Chapter 2

Definitions and Delimitations: What Is the Priesthood?

*B*efore going further, let us define the word *priesthood*. It is the power and authority of God that has always existed and will continue to exist without end. God created and governs the heavens and the earth by this power. Through this power, He brings to pass "the immortality and eternal life of man" (Moses 1:39; see also D&C 84:35–38). In mortality, priesthood is the power and authority that God gives to man to act in all things necessary for the salvation of God's children. The blessings of the priesthood are available to all who receive the gospel.[12]

The priesthood is sometimes referred to as the holy priesthood, or the Melchizedek Priesthood; however, neither of these titles is its complete or original name. The true (or original) name of the priesthood was revealed to Joseph Smith in 1835: "Why [it] is called the Melchizedek Priesthood is because Melchizedek was such a great high priest. Before his day it was called the Holy Priesthood, after the Order of the Son of God" (D&C 107:2–3).

This accurate and more expansive name is interesting, considering recent reemphasis in the Church where our leaders, especially President Russell M. Nelson, have counseled us to use the proper and full name of the Church and thus emphasize the Savior Jesus Christ, just as the complete name of the priesthood does so perfectly. With this new emphasis

---

12. Priesthood Authority," *Handbook 2: Administering the Church* (2019), 2.1.

and prophetic direction, will we one day call the Melchizedek Priesthood by its original and more complete title, which is also referred to as "the order of *the Only Begotten Son*"? (D&C 76:57; emphasis added; see also D&C 124:123.)

It is fruitless to speculate. Regardless of future events and possibilities, let us remember why the Lord has instructed the Saints in revelation to continue to use the term *Melchizedek* rather than the complete title. "But *out of respect or reverence* to the *name of the Supreme Being*, to avoid the *too frequent repetition of his name*, they, the church, in ancient days, called that priesthood after Melchizedek, or the Melchizedek Priesthood" (D&C 107:4; emphasis added). How wise! While we seek to honor and remember our Lord and Savior, Jesus Christ, we must take care to reverence and respect Him by avoiding the "too frequent repetition of his name."

The foregoing definitions and doctrines are perhaps familiar to most Church members, and I was certainly conversant with these explanations from my teenaged years. However, since that time, my understanding regarding the priesthood has grown, thanks to many wise leaders and instructors. I always knew that "all" members were able to access "all" the blessings of the priesthood, but I had never thought of (or had heard of) actual ways in which women do indeed receive and exercise priesthood authority and power. (We will get to these in the next chapter.) Looking back, I realize that I often gave students several inaccurate explanations as to why women were not given priesthood authority, as I supposed. Some of these faulty explanations, opinions, and speculations (including those that I have heard from others) are as follows:

1. The Spiritual Superiority Excuse: "Women are so much more spiritual than men."

The errant reasoning behind this excuse is that men are some sort of spiritual brutes, that their only hope for salvation is to be given a rigid, lower law structure (which strangely comes in the form of the priesthood) so that they might somehow be persuaded, directed, compelled, or guilted into doing their duty. Now, I am willing to concede that perhaps in some instances there does seem to be an inherent nature in many women that is more spiritual or divine than men, that these women perhaps have an added measure of instinctive and nurturing character, and that men are somewhat more mechanical, analytical, and perhaps not as in touch with their feelings. Surely this is an odd reason for believing that men are the only ones who need the priesthood.

As I have pondered this theory over the years, I have found that it has flaws that insult reason, unnecessarily belittle men, and even contradict divine truths found in scripture. First, the priesthood, especially the Melchizedek Priesthood, is not a lower law priesthood, though this might be the case in a limited sense with the preparatory Aaronic Priesthood. No, God created this divine and universal power by which worlds are created. Saving ordinances and miraculous healings come through this unspeakable power. "The power and authority of the higher, or Melchizedek Priesthood, is to hold the keys of all the spiritual blessings of the church—to have the privilege of receiving the mysteries of the kingdom of heaven, to have the heavens opened unto them, to commune with the general assembly and church of the Firstborn, and to enjoy the communion and presence of God the Father, and Jesus the mediator of the new covenant" (D&C 107:18–19).

No, priesthood authority should never be viewed as training wheels for an apparently spiritually deprived group of novices. This logic just doesn't add up. Other scriptures worth noting: "God is no respecter of persons" (Acts 10:34; D&C 1:35). We also read that God "inviteth them all to come unto him and partake of his goodness; and he denieth none that come unto him, black and white, bond and free, male and female; and he remembereth the heathen; and *all are alike unto God*, both Jew and Gentile" (2 Nephi 26:33; emphasis added). Reason, logic, scripture, and the Spirit of Christ within each of us bears witness to truth, which can help us see the fallacy of this inept argument.

2. The Gender Role Excuse: "Men hold the priesthood, women have babies."

Now, that may sound insensitive, but I have been shocked to see this excuse portrayed and even stated in this exact way. I choose to leave the wording of this excuse as such, only to reflect actual attitudes that I have seen with some people in the Church. This idea does have some merit in that the basic components are true, but it is obviously an over-generalization. Furthermore, this excuse compartmentalizes certain roles while minimalizing, if not outright forgetting, other important roles as well. Do men not participate in the procreative process, albeit in a different way than women? Not to mention what has been taught in the family proclamation about a variety of roles and duties that both men and women each have been given. The family proclamation states that

> Parents have a sacred duty to rear their children in love and righteousness, to provide for their physical and spiritual needs, and to teach them to love and serve one another, observe the commandments of God, and be law-abiding citizens wherever they live. . . . By divine design, fathers are to preside over their families in love and righteousness and are responsible to provide the necessities of life and protection for their families. Mothers are primarily responsible for the nurture of their children. In these sacred responsibilities, fathers and mothers are obligated to help one another as equal partners.[13]

Elder M. Russell Ballard taught,

> Let us never forget that we are the sons and daughters of God, *equal in His sight with differing responsibilities and capabilities* assigned by Him and given access to His priesthood power. . . . women come to earth with unique spiritual gifts and propensities. This is particularly true when it comes to children and families and the well-being and nurturing of others. . . . Men and women have different gifts, different strengths, and different points of view and inclinations. That is one of the fundamental reasons we need each other.[14]

Part of this equality, as we shall see in the next chapter, includes the fact that both men and women participate in and with priesthood authority, both in different and sometimes similar ways. The priesthood is not just for men.

3.   The Unknowable Mystery Excuse: "Leave it alone, have faith. We will learn more someday."

Now, perhaps there is some truth in this one. The scriptures do teach us to "trust in the Lord with all thine heart; and lean not unto thine own understanding" (Proverbs 3:5–6), and God has stated clearly, "My

---

13. "The Family: A Proclamation to the World," *Ensign* or *Liahona*, Nov. 2010, 129.
14. Ballard, "Men and Women in the Work of the Lord"; emphasis added.

ways [are] higher than your ways, and my thoughts [are higher] than your thoughts" (Isaiah 55:9). But are these scriptures relevant to the question at hand? It is hazardous when we claim to know something in the gospel or the Church that we really don't know. However, it is an equally great hazard to claim that we don't know something when in reality we do. Elder Ballard gave this cautionary counsel:

> Gone are the days when a student asked an honest question and a teacher responded, 'Don't worry about it!' Gone are the days when a student raised a sincere concern and a teacher bore his or her testimony as a response intended to avoid the issue. It is perfectly all right to say, 'I do not know.' However, once that is said, you have a responsibility to find the best answers to thoughtful questions your students ask.[15]

In the same talk, Elder Ballard went on to say (and this applies to the previous three excuses):

> Let me warn you not to pass along faith-promoting or *unsubstantiated rumors or outdated understandings and explanations of our doctrine and practices from the past.* It is always wise to make it a practice to study the words of the living prophets and apostles; *keep updated on current Church issues, policies, and statements . . .* and consult the works of recognized, thoughtful, and faithful LDS scholars to *ensure you do not teach things that are untrue, out of date, or odd and quirky.*[16]

The real fallacy with all these excuses is that they avoid the central issue which we seek to explore, that women can and do receive and can exercise priesthood authority.

To Have or to Hold?

Now, before we get to the next chapter and the central issue at hand, lets dispense with a few disclaimers centered on verbiage and semantics relating to priesthood in the Church. Can women *hold* priesthood authority? This issue has been made clear by many prophetic voices in the Church. Usually the word *hold* is employed when talking about those

---

15. M. Russell Ballard, "An Evening with Elder M. Russell Ballard," CES Fireside, broadcast Feb. 26, 2016. See churchofjesuschrist.org.
16. Ballard, "An Evening with Elder M. Russell Ballard"; emphasis added.

leaders who hold priesthood keys, such as a bishop or stake president. In fact, very few men hold keys in our local units. However, another loose way in which the term *hold* is often used is when referring to priesthood *holders*. Usually what is meant here is young men or adult males who have been *ordained* to offices within the Aaronic or Melchizedek Priesthoods.

It might be worth mentioning a few terms that are often employed when discussing certain functions of the priesthood. We *confer* Aaronic and Melchizedek Priesthood. We *ordain* to offices in those priesthoods, and we *set apart* to callings within the priesthood. (This definition will become more meaningful and important in the next chapter.)

In the early days of this last dispensation, there was not always a distinction between the terms *ordain* and *set apart*. For example, the Lord gave a revelation in the Doctrine and Covenants through Joseph Smith to his wife Emma, calling her to do several important things in the Church. The specific wording of part of this revelation is worth noting: "And *the office of thy calling* shall be for a comfort unto my servant, Joseph Smith, Jun., thy husband, in his afflictions, with consoling words, in the spirit of meekness. And thou shalt go with him at the time of his going, and be unto him for a scribe, while there is no one to be a scribe for him, that I may send my servant, Oliver Cowdery, whithersoever I will. And *thou shalt be ordained* under his hand to expound scriptures, and to exhort the church, according as it shall be given thee by my Spirit" (D&C 25:5–7; emphasis added).

Lest any think that Emma was *ordained* to an *office* of the priesthood, though the verses do indeed contain these words, the footnote to the word *ordain* clarifies the intended meaning: to be *set apart*. There are other examples in the revelations and statements in the early days of the restoration where the word *ordain* is used to mean *set apart*.

In our dispensation, there are four offices of the Aaronic Priesthood to which one can be ordained; namely, deacon, teacher, priest, and bishop. Within the Melchizedek Priesthood there are five offices: elder, high priest, patriarch, seventy, and apostle.[17] A few examples of *callings* in

---

17. In older Church publications, *President of the Church* is sometimes listed as a sixth Melchizedek Priesthood office. However, contemporary Church publications refer to this as a calling rather than an ordained priesthood office. Both the *Guide to the Scriptures* and the current edition of the Bible Dictionary mention only five Melchizedek Priesthood offices.

the priesthood include, but are not limited to, elder's quorum president, stake president, and counselors in presidencies.

Several years ago, I was called as the bishop of a young single adult ward. Although the stake president first *ordained* me to the office of bishop in the Aaronic Priesthood, he also needed to *set me apart* as the bishop of the specific ward in which I was called to serve. Thus, bishop is both an *office* and a *calling*. The same could be said of patriarch: it is an office of the Melchizedek Priesthood, yet a patriarch must also be set apart as the patriarch of the stake in which he labors.

Although women do not *hold* priesthood authority, meaning either keys being given to them or being *ordained* to an office in the Aaronic or Melchizedek Priesthood, women receive priesthood authority and exercise its power in various ways which we will explore now in the next chapter.

Chapter 3

Yes, Women Can Receive Priesthood Authority

We are not accustomed to speaking of women having the authority of the priesthood in their Church callings, but what other authority can it be?[18]

—President Dallin H. Oaks

We finally arrive now at the central focus of this book: women can and do indeed participate in the priesthood, are given priesthood authority, function under priesthood authority, exercise priesthood authority, and have in mortality and will have in eternity, if they so choose, the power and authority of the holy priesthood. In this chapter, we will look at seven ways this is so.[19] It is hoped that the reader will carefully explore the scriptures cited herein and the prophetic voices that teach and bear witness to these powerful truths. It is the author's belief that as members of the Church become more familiar with and conversant in these truths, many potential misunderstandings, frustrations, and pains will be avoided. How important it is to be "instructed more perfectly in . . . principle, in doctrine, in the law of the gospel, in all things that

---

18. Dallin H. Oaks, "The Keys and Authority of the Priesthood," *Ensign*, May 2014.

19. This chapter is based on lectures I have given in BYU religion classes for more than a decade. I openly acknowledge that some of my BYU students may have shared ideas gained in my class in other forums in the intervening years. I also acknowledge and am aware of similar lists that have been put forth in recent months and years by other individuals.

pertain unto the kingdom of God" (D&C 88:78) and all this for "the perfecting of the saints, for the work of the ministry, for the edifying of the body of Christ: Till *we all come in the unity of the faith*, and of the knowledge of the Son of God, unto a perfect man, *unto the measure of the stature of the fulness of Christ*" (Ephesians 4:12–13; emphasis added).

1. Women Can Receive and Exercise Priesthood Authority in Their Church Callings

One of the most plain and frequent ways in which women receive priesthood authority is in their Church callings. In the Doctrine and Covenants we learn that *"All other authorities or offices in the church are appendages to this* [Melchizedek] *priesthood. . . .* The Melchizedek Priesthood holds the right of presidency, and has *power and authority over all the offices in the church* in all ages of the world, to administer in spiritual things" (D&C 107:5–8; emphasis added). Any calling, office, or position that anyone holds in this Church comes through and is given by virtue of the Melchizedek Priesthood. Callings in the Primary organization or Relief Society, for instance—these are not separate authorities, functions, or callings from the priesthood. No, as we just read in Doctrine and Covenants 107:5, "all . . . offices in the church are appendages" or a literal part of the holy priesthood.

A memorable and recent teaching on this specific point of doctrine was made very clear by President Oaks when he said,

> We are not accustomed to speaking of *women having the authority of the priesthood in their Church callings, but what other authority can it be?* When a woman—young or old—is set apart to preach the gospel as a full-time missionary, *she is given priesthood authority* to perform a priesthood function. The same is true when a woman is set apart to function as an officer or teacher in a Church organization under the direction of one who holds the keys of the priesthood. Whoever functions in an office or calling received from one who holds priesthood keys exercises priesthood authority in performing her or his assigned duties.[20]

Elder Ballard has given a second witness to this principle, instructing that women not only can receive priesthood authority in their callings,

---

20. Oaks, "The Keys and Authority of the Priesthood"; emphasis added.

but they *exercise* it as well: "Those who have priesthood keys . . . literally make it possible for *all who serve* faithfully under their direction *to exercise priesthood authority and have access to priesthood power*."[21]

Likewise, Elder Neal L. Anderson has taught the same principle, adding a clarifying detail:

> We know that the keys of the priesthood, held by members of the First Presidency and Quorum of the Twelve Apostles, direct the work of the Lord upon the earth. Specific priesthood keys are conferred upon stake presidents and bishops for their geographic responsibilities. And they call men and women by revelation who are *sustained and set apart to exercise delegated authority to teach and administer*.[22]

From these three prophetic witnesses, it is clear that women may receive and exercise priesthood authority in their Church callings. This applies even with callings given to the young women of the Church: "A *young woman called* and set apart to serve in a class presidency *functions in her calling with delegated priesthood authority*."[23]

This delegated priesthood authority is not a lesser portion of the priesthood. No, it is on par with and the same as any other individual who receives a calling—man or woman. Sister Diane L. Mangum has said,

> When a bishop places his hands on the head of a Beehive class president, *it is with the full power of the priesthood that he gives her the delegated authority* to lead her class. Her calling to *serve is no less potent or real than that of the Sunday School president, the Relief Society president, or any other position in the ward*.[24]

When it comes to callings in the Church, it should thus be noted that both "women and men are delegated power and authority by those who

---

21. Ballard, "Men and Women in the Work of the Lord"; emphasis added.
22. Neal L. Anderson, "Power in the Priesthood," *Ensign*, Nov. 2013; emphasis added.
23. Carol F. McConkie, "'Called to Lead': The Influence of Young Women Class Presidencies," *Church News*, Mar. 21, 2016; emphasis added. See churchofjesuschrist.org.
24. Diane L. Mangum, "Young Women and the Blessings of the Priesthood," *Ensign*, May 1993; emphasis added.

hold priesthood keys."[25] There is no contest, there is no need to worry or complain. There is no disadvantage or advantage to either men or women. When it comes to priesthood authority in our callings, we are essentially all on the same standing. Ultimately, all power and authority resting in the priesthood goes back to the Savior Himself:

> Jesus Christ holds all the keys of the priesthood pertaining to His Church. He has conferred upon each of His Apostles all the keys that pertain to the kingdom of God on earth. The senior living Apostle, the President of the Church, is the only person on earth authorized to exercise all priesthood keys (see D&C 107:91–92). . . . [He then] delegates priesthood keys to other priesthood leaders so they can preside in their areas of responsibility. . . . Auxiliary presidents and their counselors do not receive keys. They receive delegated authority to function in their callings.[26]

2. Women Exercise Priesthood Authority and Receive Priesthood Power in the Temple

Another way women receive and exercise priesthood authority can be seen in the inspired and glorious work that is done in the temples of the Church, even the house of the Lord. It is in the temple that women not only exercise priesthood authority, but they likewise receive priesthood power.

President Ballard teaches that, "the endowment is literally a gift of power. All who enter the house of the Lord officiate in *the ordinances of the priesthood. This applies to men and women alike.*"[27]

He went on to say, "When *men and women* go to the temple, *they are both endowed with the same power, which is priesthood power.* While the authority of the priesthood is directed through priesthood keys, and priesthood keys are held only by worthy men, access to the power and the blessings of the priesthood is available to all of God's children."[28]

---

25. Barbara Morgan Gardner, "I Have So Much to Learn about the Priesthood," *Ensign*, Mar. 2019.

26. Linda K. Burton, "Priesthood Power Available to All," Women's Conference, Brigham Young University, May 2, 2013. See also *Ensign*, June 2014, and churchofjesuschrist.org.

27. Ballard, "Men and Women in the Work of the Lord"; emphasis added.

28. Ibid.

Elder John A. Widtsoe of the Quorum of the Twelve Apostles wrote,

> The priesthood is for the benefit of all members of the Church. We have no greater claim than women upon the blessings that issue from the priesthood and accompany its possession. A woman does not hold the priesthood, but she is a partaker of the blessings of the priesthood. *This is made clear, as an example, in the temple service of the Church. The ordinances of the temple are distinctly of priesthood character, yet women have access to all of them,* and the highest blessings of the temple are conferred only upon a man and his wife jointly.[29]

President Dallin H. Oaks has also taught that "the sacred work that sisters do in the temple" in helping to perform priesthood ordinances is done "under the keys held by the temple president," and that this is the one rare occasion where a woman can and does use priesthood authority they are given to "officiate in a priesthood ordinance."[30]

The words of President Joseph Fielding Smith are also helpful in this matter:

> While the sisters have not been given the priesthood, it has not been conferred upon them, *that does not mean that the Lord has not given unto them authority.* . . . A person may have *authority given* to him, *or a sister to her,* to do certain things in the Church *that are binding and absolutely necessary for our salvation, such as the work that our sisters do in the house of the Lord.* They have authority given unto them to do some great and wonderful things, sacred unto the Lord, and binding just as thoroughly as are the blessings that are given by the men who hold the priesthood.[31]

3. Women Can Enter into the Patriarchal Order of the Priesthood via Temple Marriage

Women not only may receive and exercise priesthood authority, but they also actually enter into an order of the priesthood. Simply put, not

---

29. John A. Widtsoe, *Priesthood and Church Government* (Salt Lake City: Deseret Book, 1954), p. 83; emphasis added.
30. Oaks, "The Keys and Authority of the Priesthood."
31. Joseph Fielding Smith, "Relief Society—an Aid to the Priesthood," *The Relief Society Magazine*, Jan. 1959, 4; see also Oaks, "The Keys and Authority of the Priesthood."

only men, but women also, enter this priesthood order, which is otherwise known as temple marriage. Often, we think of just two orders of the priesthood because of this scripture: "There are, in the church, two priesthoods, namely, the Melchizedek and Aaronic, including the Levitical Priesthood" (D&C 107:1). However, eight years after this revelation, in a discourse given during the construction of the Nauvoo Temple, Joseph Smith declared that knowledge of another priesthood order, the *patriarchal order* (or authority), would be revealed in the temple.[32]

These verses, now in the Doctrine and Covenants and given in 1843, are helpful in clarifying this point of doctrine: "In the celestial glory there are three heavens or degrees; And in order to obtain the highest, a man must enter into *this order of the priesthood . . . meaning the new and everlasting covenant of marriage*" (D&C 131:1–2; emphasis added). From this time forward, Joseph Smith declared on several occasions that "there are three grand orders of priesthood," mainly, "the Aaronic, the Melchizedek, and the *patriarchal authority*. Go to and *finish the temple*," he said, "and God will fill it with power, and *you will then receive more knowledge concerning this priesthood*."[33]

Elder Bruce R. McConkie confirms this teaching and clarifies what this priesthood order specifically is: "We can enter an *order of the priesthood* named *the new and everlasting covenant of marriage*, named also *the patriarchal order*."[34]

President Benson likewise has taught, "The *order of priesthood* spoken of in the scriptures is sometimes referred to as *the patriarchal order*. But this order is otherwise described in modern revelation as an *order of family government.* This order of priesthood *can only be entered into by going to our Father's house.* I hope you would teach this truth about the temple to your children and your grandchildren."[35]

An interesting scriptural phrase that is helpful to know is "the fulness of the priesthood." Now some might think that this refers to the Melchizedek Priesthood. This is not entirely so. True, the Melchizedek

---

32. The patriarchal priesthood should not be confused with the priesthood office and calling of the patriarch.

33. See *Teachings of the Prophet Joseph Smith* (Salt Lake City: Deseret Book, 1977), 166, 180, 308, and 322; emphasis added.

34. Bruce R. McConkie, "The Doctrine of the Priesthood," *Ensign*, May 1982, 33–34; emphasis added.

35. Ezra Taft Benson, "What I Hope You Will Teach Your Children about the Temple," *Ensign*, Aug. 1985; emphasis added.

Priesthood is sometimes referred to as the "higher" or "greater" priesthood (D&C 84:19; 107:18), but *the fulness of the priesthood* is a phrase that relates to and is synonymous with the patriarchal order. "For there is not a place found on earth that he may come to and restore again that which was lost . . . even the *fulness of the priesthood*" (D&C 124:28; emphasis added). Not only do both men and women enter this order, but they must also enter it together. President Boyd K. Packer has said, "The highest ordinance in the House of the Lord, *a man and woman receive together and equally or not at all.*"[36]

On another occasion, President Packer tenderly instructed, "Those who tell you that in the kingdom of God a woman's lot is less than that of the man know nothing of the love . . . that the worthy man has for his wife. He cannot have his priesthood, *not the fulness of it*, without her."[37]

Sister Sheri Dew has taught, "Most significantly, the *fulness of the priesthood* contained in the highest ordinances of the house of the Lord can only be received by a man and woman together."[38]

President M. Russell Ballard has likewise stated, "Just as a woman cannot conceive a child without a man, so a *man cannot fully exercise the power of the priesthood to establish an eternal family without a woman.*"[39]

Elder Bruce R. McConkie further explains, "In the true Patriarchal Order man . . . cannot attain a fulness of joy here or of eternal reward hereafter alone. Woman stands at his side *a joint-inheritor with him in the fulness of all things.* Exaltation and eternal increase is her lot as well as his . . . Godhood is not for men only; it is for men and women together."[40]

Recently, Elder Dale G. Renlund wrote, "A woman participates *in the fulness of the Melchizedek Priesthood through temple sealing* to a worthy Melchizedek Priesthood holder."[41]

Although it is doctrinally correct to discuss temple marriage between a man and a woman as the *patriarchal order* of the priesthood (as we have

---

36. Boyd K. Packer, *Things of the Soul* (Salt Lake City: Bookcraft, 1996), 173; emphasis added.

37. Boyd K. Packer, "The Circle of Sisters," *Ensign*, Nov. 1980; emphasis added.

38. Sheri L. Dew, "It Is Not Good for Man or Woman to Be Alone," *Ensign*, Nov. 2001, 12; emphasis added.

39. M. Russell Ballard, "'This Is My Work and Glory,'" *Ensign*, May 2013, 19; emphasis added.

40. Bruce R. McConkie, *Mormon Doctrine*, 2nd ed. (Salt Lake City: Bookcraft, 1979), 844; emphasis added.

41. Renlund and Renlund, *The Melchizedek Priesthood*; emphasis added.

herein established), care should be taken not to stretch this doctrine too far. The patriarchal order is not another, completely different priesthood. It is *an order of* the priesthood.

President Boyd K. Packer gave the following wise caution:

> There are references to a patriarchal priesthood. *The patriarchal order is not a third, separate priesthood.* Whatever relates to the patriarchal order is embraced in the Melchizedek Priesthood. 'All other authorities or offices in the church are appendages to [the Melchizedek] priesthood [D&C 107:5].' The patriarchal order is a part of the Melchizedek Priesthood which enables endowed and worthy men to preside over their posterity in time and eternity.[42]

The same could be said of the Aaronic, which is an appendage, or part of the higher priesthood (D&C 107:14).

4.   Women May Receive and Be Given Priesthood Authority Eternally

Women not only receive and exercise priesthood authority here in mortality, but if they are faithful, they also can and will receive priesthood authority eternally. President M. Russell Ballard has declared, "In the *eternal perspective*, both the *procreative power* and the *priesthood power* are *shared by husband and wife.*"[43]

Celestial marriage in the temple is for time and all eternity. Furthermore, it has been revealed, as we have stated previously, that temple marriage is a priesthood order that women can enter, even the fulness of the priesthood for all eternity. Not only will women be in this order of the priesthood for all eternity, but they will likewise be given authority in the priesthood for all eternity as well.

President Joseph Fielding Smith declared,

> There is nothing in the teachings of the gospel which declares that men are superior to women. . . . The most noble, exalting calling of all is that which has been given to women as the mothers of men. Women do not

---

42. Boyd K. Packer, "What Every Elder Should Know—and Every Sister as Well: A Primer on Principles of Priesthood Government," *Ensign*, Feb. 1993; emphasis added.
43. Ballard, "'This Is My Work and Glory'"; emphasis added.

hold the priesthood [meaning priesthood keys or an ordained office], but if they are faithful and true, *they will become priestesses and queens in the kingdom of God, and that implies that they will be given authority.*[44]

Now, some might ask what this authority is of which President Smith is speaking. It is true he does not specifically clarify, though the statement in the sentence is in context of the priesthood. However, to quote President Oaks once again, "We are not accustomed to speaking of *women having the authority of the priesthood in their Church callings, but what other authority can it be?*"[45]

5.   Women Can Receive All the Blessings of the Priesthood

Another way in which women receive the priesthood is that they can receive all of the blessings that issue from the priesthood. President Oaks said, "Priesthood power blesses all of us. Priesthood keys direct women as well as men, and priesthood ordinances and priesthood authority pertain to women as well as men."[46]

Sheri Dew has also taught,

> My young sisters, some will try to persuade you that because you are not ordained to the priesthood you have been shortchanged. They are simply wrong, and they do not understand the gospel of Jesus Christ. The blessings of the priesthood are available to every righteous man and woman . . . The power of the priesthood heals, protects, and inoculates all of the righteous against the powers of darkness. . . . Sisters, we as women are not diminished by priesthood power, we are magnified by it. I know this is true, for I have experienced it again and again.[47]

President Joseph Fielding Smith likewise taught, "There is no exaltation in the kingdom of God without the fulness of the priesthood . . . we all know that *the blessings of the priesthood are not confined to men alone. These blessings are also poured out upon our wives and daughters and upon all*

44.   Joseph Fielding Smith, *Doctrines of Salvation*, comp. Bruce R. McConkie, 3 vols. (Salt Lake City: Bookcraft, 1954–56), 3:178; emphasis added.

45.   Oaks, "The Keys and Authority of the Priesthood"; emphasis added.

46.   Ibid.; emphasis added.

47.   Dew, "It Is Not Good for Man or Woman to Be Alone," 12; emphasis added.

the faithful women of the Church . . . The Lord offers to his daughters every spiritual gift and blessing that can be obtained by his sons."[48]

6. Women Can Access Authority and Power through Desires, Faith, and Righteousness

Priesthood is the power of God. In a very broad sense, anyone who receives the power of God, in any form, receives priesthood power. The Holy Ghost is one such influence that allows Church members to receive this power in their lives. In the scriptures we are taught, "But *ye shall receive power, after that the Holy Ghost is come* upon you" (Acts 1:8; emphasis added). Preliminary and prerequisite to receiving the Holy Ghost is the demonstration and exercise of *faith* on behalf of the recipient.[49]

In Nephi's words, "And it came to pass after I, Nephi, having heard all the words of my father, concerning the things which he saw in a vision, and also the things which he spake by *the power of the Holy Ghost, which power he received by faith* on the Son of God" (1 Nephi 10:17; emphasis added).

In addition to *faith* being a gateway to access God's power, *desires* likewise allow us to access this power and qualify us to help build his kingdom here on earth. In the Doctrine and Covenants we read, "Therefore, O ye that embark in the service of God, see that ye serve him with all your heart, might, mind and strength, that ye may stand blameless before God at the last day. *Therefore, if ye have desires to serve God ye are called to the work*" (D&C 4:2–3; emphasis added).

We are further instructed in modern revelation to "Seek not to declare my word, but first seek to obtain my word, and then shall your tongue be loosed; *then, if you desire, you shall have my Spirit and my word, yea, the power of God* unto the convincing of men" (D&C 11:21; emphasis added).

If priesthood power is in reality the power of God, then it stands to reason that any Church member, male or female, who desires to do good and exercises faith receives the Holy Ghost. All of these allow any of us (in a very broad sense) to access priesthood power and authority to teach, preach, and to inspire others. Some Christian churches might misunderstand this type of access to God's power, thinking that formal priesthood

---

48. Smith, *Doctrines of Salvation*; emphasis added.
49. Articles of Faith 1:4; emphasis added.

authority and priesthood keys are therefore unnecessary. Such a conclusion would surely be contrary to restored gospel truth.

7. Future of Women and the Priesthood Here in Mortality

Are there other ways in which Latter-day Saint women will one day be able to receive priesthood authority in the future? Perhaps even in ways that have yet to be revealed? Only time will tell. We do believe "all that God has revealed, all that He does now reveal, and we believe that *He will yet reveal many great and important things*."[50] The Lord is not done with his work.

Elder Uchtdorf has said,

> Sometimes we think of the Restoration of the gospel as something that is complete, already behind us—Joseph Smith translated the Book of Mormon, he received priesthood keys, the Church was organized. In reality, the *Restoration is an ongoing process*; we are living in it right now."[51] He went on to say, "The *exciting developments of today* are part of that long-foretold period of preparation that will culminate in the glorious Second Coming of our Savior, Jesus Christ.

President Nelson, at the dedication of the Rome Temple said, "This is a hinge point in the history of the Church. Things are going to move forward at an accelerated pace, of which this is a part . . . . The Church is going to have an unprecedented future, unparalleled; *we're just building up to what's ahead now.*"[52]

In the Doctrine and Covenants we learn, "And also those to whom these commandments were given, might have power to lay the foundation of this church, and *to bring it forth out of obscurity and out of darkness*, the only true and living church upon the face of the whole earth" (D&C 1:30;

---

50. Articles of Faith 1:9; emphasis added.

51. Dieter F. Uchtdorf, "Are You Sleeping through the Restoration?" *Ensign*, May 2014; emphasis added.

52. Tad Walch, "Rome Temple a 'hinge point' in Latter-day Saint history, President Nelson says as he leaves Italy," *Deseret News*, Mar. 11, 2019; emphasis added. See deseretnews.com.

emphasis added). Not only is the restoration unfinished, but likewise "the Church has not yet fully emerged from darkness and obscurity"[53]

So, are there any future ways in which women in the Church will receive the priesthood, ways that are not yet revealed but one day might be? If such a thing were to happen, it would not come because of social pressure or efforts to coerce those with priesthood keys. It would come, as it always does, because of revelation from heaven given to those with priesthood keys. How might this happen? We can only guess in ignorance and speculate with the uncertainty of limited perspective. Wisdom and prudence tells us to wait and be patient, to live faithfully and trust in the Lord's timing and purposes. Perhaps our time and efforts would be best spent implementing what God has already revealed. However, a verse regarding these matters is found in the Doctrine and Covenants. "High priests after the order of the Melchizedek Priesthood have a right to officiate in their own standing, under the direction of the presidency, in administering spiritual things, and also *in the office of* an elder, priest (of the Levitical order), teacher, deacon, and *member*" (D&C 107:10; emphasis added).

The wording here is interesting. Could there perhaps be another priesthood office, ordained or not, even that of "member?" Or does this mean that all members will someday be able to access all the blessings of the priesthood? Might there be further divine clarification on what this term "member" means in the context of the aforementioned priesthood offices? Might we learn in the future the connection that women could have with such a potential priesthood office?

There is precedent of God revealing to his servants deeper clarifications on extant revelations in the Doctrine and Covenants regarding the meaning and scope of priesthood authority. In the 1980s and 1990s, the Melchizedek Priesthood office of Seventy was clarified and modified. President Hinckley said, "Now in the ongoing of this work, *administrative changes sometimes occur. The doctrine remains constant.* But from time to time *there are organizational and administrative changes made under provisions set forth in the revelations.*"[54]

---

53. Bruce L. Olsen, "Out of Obscurity and Out of Darkness." Adapted from a talk given at Women's Conference on May 1, 1998, at Brigham Young University. See churchofjesuschrist.org.

54. Gordon B. Hinckley, "This Work Is Concerned with People," *Ensign*, May 1995, 51.

One such provision, President Hinckley said, was this verse in the Doctrine and Covenants: "And also other seventy, until seven times seventy, if the labor in the vineyard of necessity requires it" (D&C 107:96). He then said, "With these respective quorums in place, we have established a pattern under which the Church may grow to any size with an organization of Area Presidencies and Area Authority Seventies, chosen and working across the world according to need."

It could be argued that the changes that were made more closely parallel the scriptural wording and intent in section 107 of the Doctrine and Covenants than perhaps what was done previously. Said President Hinckley, "This, I submit, is the inspired genius of this the Lord's work. The organization can grow and multiply in numbers, as it surely will."[55]

Will more inspired changes take place in the future, especially those that impact women in the Church? Only time will tell.

Conclusion

It is hoped that all of us, both men and women in the Church, will realize how much we need each other. We all have important, divine roles to fulfill, and all of us are entitled to all the blessings that issue from our Heavenly Father's inestimable power known as the priesthood. True, it is that women do not *hold* priesthood, meaning *it is not conferred upon them in an office* of either the Aaronic or Melchizedek Priesthoods. However, it is clear that women *receive and are given priesthood authority* in their callings. They *exercise priesthood authority* in administering sacred temple ordinances. They can enter an order of the priesthood called the patriarchal order, even the fulness of the priesthood through temple marriage. And finally, if faithful and true, women will receive priesthood authority eternally as queens and priestesses in the celestial kingdom of our Heavenly Father.

Over the years, I have had several students, mostly female, share the following sentiment: "Sometimes I wonder if I am the person God intended me to be. Maybe I should have been born in a different time, or as a different person, or even with a different gender." I often have shared the following quotation at the conclusion of lessons where we have discussed sacred doctrines and principles relative to our own individual worth and place in God's eternal plan:

---

55. Hinckley, "This Work Is Concerned with People," 51.

I have a conviction deep down in my heart that *we are exactly what we should be*, each one of us, except as we may have altered that pattern by deviating from the laws of God here in mortality. I have convinced myself that *we all have those peculiar attributes, characteristics, and abilities which are essential for us to possess in order that we may fulfill the full purpose of our creation* here upon this earth. Once again, *that allotment* which has come to us from God *is a sacred allotment*. It is something of which we should be proud, each one of us in our own right, and not wish that we had somebody else's allotment. Our greatest success comes from being ourselves. I think that we can console ourselves best by believing that whatever is our allotment in life, *whatever is our call in the priesthood* [and remember we all can receive, exercise, and access priesthood power and authority in various ways], the Lord has been wise and just, and I might add, merciful, in giving to us that which we need to accomplish the particular purpose of our call.[56]

To conclude this chapter, I wish to direct the attention of the reader to this wonderful, insightful, and profound parable that was shared by President Boyd K. Packer. The parable is lengthy, but in my opinion, it illustrates, in an excellent way, the principles we are discussing in this book. It not only frames and summarizes what I have sought to teach in this chapter, but it also introduces several related and important concepts in the upcoming chapters.

 Once a man received as his inheritance two keys. The first key, he was told, would open a vault which he must protect at all cost. The second key was to a safe within the vault which contained a priceless treasure. He was to open this safe and freely use the precious things which were stored therein. He was warned that many would seek to rob him of his inheritance. He was promised that if he used the treasure worthily, it would be replenished and never be diminished, not in all eternity. He would be tested. If he used it to benefit others, his own blessings and joy would increase. The man went alone to the vault. His first key opened the door. He tried to unlock the treasure with the other key, but he could not, for there were two locks on the safe. His key alone would not open it. No matter how he tried, he could not open it. He was puzzled. He had been given the keys. He knew the treasure was rightfully his. He had obeyed instructions, but he could not open the safe.

---

56. Henry D. Moyle, in Conference Report, Oct. 1952, 71–72.

In due time, there came a woman into the vault. She, too, held a key. It was noticeably different from the key he held. Her key fit the other lock. It humbled him to learn that he could not obtain his rightful inheritance without her. They made a covenant that together they would open the treasure and, as instructed, he would watch over the vault and protect it; she would watch over the treasure. She was not concerned that . . . he held two keys, for his full purpose was to see that she was safe as she watched over that which was most precious to them both.

Together they opened the safe and partook of their inheritance. They rejoiced for, as promised, it replenished itself. With great joy they found that they could pass the treasure on to their children. Each could receive a full measure, undiminished to the last generation. Perhaps some few of their posterity would not find a companion who possessed the complementary key, or one worthy and willing to keep the covenants relating to the treasure. Nevertheless, if they kept the commandments, they would not be denied even the smallest blessing. Because some tempted them to misuse their treasure, they were careful to teach their children about keys and covenants.

There came, in due time, among their posterity some few who were deceived or jealous or selfish because one was given two keys and another only one. "Why," the selfish ones reasoned, "cannot the treasure be mine alone to use as I desire?"

Some tried to reshape the key they had been given to resemble the other key. Perhaps, they thought, it would then fit both locks. And so it was that the safe was closed to them. Their reshaped keys were useless, and their inheritance was lost. Those who received the treasure with gratitude and obeyed the laws concerning it knew joy without bounds through time and all eternity.[57]

---

57. Boyd K. Packer, "For Time and All Eternity," *Ensign*, Nov. 1993, 23.

Chapter 4

Yes, There Is a
Mother in Heaven

It is a serious thing to live in a society of possible gods and goddesses, to remember that the dullest and most uninteresting person you talk to may one day be a creature which, if you saw it now, you would be strongly tempted to worship, or else a horror and a corruption such as you now meet, if at all, only in a nightmare. All day long we are, in some degree, helping each other to one or other of these destinations.[58]

—C. S. Lewis

*I*n this chapter, we focus on a unique and distinctive LDS doctrine, mainly, that there is a Mother in Heaven. This doctrine is important to understand regarding the main thrust of this book and is an extension of the reality that women not only participate in and with priesthood power and authority here in mortality, but may, if they so choose, also receive this power eternally. Previously we have established that "if they

---

58. C. S. Lewis, "The Weight of Glory," a sermon preached at the Church of St. Mary the Virgin, Oxford, on June 8, 1941, and published most recently in C. S. Lewis Essay Collection: *Faith, Christianity, and the Church.* See Mere C. S. Lewis at merecslewis.blogspot.com; accessed July 30, 2019.

are faithful and true, *they will become priestesses and queens in the kingdom of God, and that implies that they will be given authority.*"[59]

Another way to say this is that women, like worthy exalted men, may become "gods, because they have no end; therefore shall they be from everlasting to everlasting, because they continue; then shall they be above all, because all things are subject unto them. Then shall they be gods, because they have all power, and the angels are subject unto them" (D&C 132:20). Furthermore, we would add that women and men alike, in simple terms, may one day become heavenly parents just like our own Heavenly Parents. President Dallin H. Oaks has said, "Our theology begins with heavenly parents. Our highest aspiration is to be like them."[60] Although the concept of Heavenly Mother is not often emphasized in the Church, it is nonetheless a true doctrine. Let us explore this concept a bit further.

The Church has recently released a wonderful essay about this topic which contains this summary declaration:

> The Church of Jesus Christ of Latter-day Saints teaches that all human beings, male and female, are beloved spirit children of heavenly parents, a Heavenly Father and a Heavenly Mother. This understanding is rooted in scriptural and prophetic teachings about the nature of God, our relationship to Deity, and the godly potential of men and women. The doctrine of a Heavenly Mother is a cherished and distinctive belief among Latter-day Saints.[61]

Elder M. Russell Ballard has taught, "We are part of a divine plan designed by Heavenly Parents who love us."[62] President Harold B. Lee has also stated, "We forget that we have a Heavenly Father and a Heavenly Mother who are even more concerned, probably, than our earthly father and mother, and that influences from beyond are constantly working to try to help us when we do all we can."[63]

In "The Family: A Proclamation to the World," issued in 1995, the First Presidency and Quorum of the Twelve Apostles declared, "Each

---

59. Smith, *Doctrines of Salvation*, 3:178; emphasis added.

60. Dallin H. Oaks, "Apostasy and Restoration," *Ensign*, May 1995, 84.

61. "Mother in Heaven," Gospel Topics Essays; see churchofjesuschrist.org.

62. M. Russell Ballard, *When Thou Art Converted: Continuing Our Search for Happiness* (Salt Lake City: Deseret Book, 2001), 62.

63. Harold B. Lee, "The Influence and Responsibility of Women," *The Relief Society Magazine*, Feb. 1964, 85.

[person] is a beloved spirit son or daughter of *heavenly parents*, and, as such, each has a divine nature and destiny."[64] This accords with what the First Presidency of the Church taught in 1909 that "all men and women are in the similitude of the *universal Father and Mother and are literally the sons and daughters of Deity*."[65]

Every now and then when I teach a lesson on this topic, various questions arise. One such question has to do with prayer and whether it would be appropriate and acceptable to pray to our Mother in Heaven. Most Latter-day Saints understand that we direct our worship to Heavenly Father, in the name of Christ, and thus do not pray to our Mother in Heaven. Thus, we follow the pattern set by Jesus Christ, who taught His disciples to "always pray unto the Father in my name" (3 Nephi 18:19–21). Latter-day Saints pray to Heavenly Father, but as President Gordon B. Hinckley has stated, "The fact that we do not pray to our Mother in Heaven in no way belittles or denigrates her."[66] Indeed, as Elder Rudger Clawson wrote, "We honor woman when we acknowledge Godhood in her eternal Prototype."[67]

Another question that students sometimes ask is worth noting. I'll occasionally have a student ask this question: "Brother Line, we sometimes talk about a Mother in Heaven, but she's never mentioned in the scriptures. I know we have one hymn that mentions her, but it is the only hymn." Actually, we have three hymns that mention Heavenly Mother (see the end of this chapter), and even the scriptures implicitly mention her at least four times.

In Genesis 2:24, it says, "Therefore shall a man leave his father and his mother and shall cleave unto his wife: and they shall be one flesh." At this point, Adam and Eve were the only man and woman on the earth, and they came from heavenly parents—direct, lineal descendants, as we have previously stated. Verse 24 says that Adam left his father *and* his mother, which refers to Heavenly Father and *Heavenly Mother*. The second place in scripture that Heavenly Mother is mentioned is in Moses 3:24. This

---

64. "The Family: A Proclamation to the World"; emphasis added.

65. Joseph Smith, John R. Winder, and Athon H. Lund, First Presidency of The Church of Jesus Christ of Latter-day Saints, "The Origin of Man," Nov. 1909; emphasis added. See also *Ensign*, Feb. 2002.

66. Gordon B. Hinckley, "Daughters of God," *Ensign*, Nov. 1991, 100.

67. Rudger Clawson, "Our Mother in Heaven," *Latter-day Saints' Millennial Star*, 72, no. 39 (Sept. 29, 1910), 620.

verse has the exact same wording: "Therefore shall a man [Adam] leave his Father [Heavenly Father] and his mother [Heavenly Mother] and cleave unto his wife [Eve] and they shall be one flesh."

Heavenly Mother is also referenced to in Ephesians 5:31–32. Earlier in Ephesians 5:22–23, Paul is talking to the Ephesian Saints about the marriage relationship. He says "wives, submit yourselves unto your own husbands as unto the Lord. The husband is the head of the wife, even as Christ is the head of the church."

Heavenly mother

After thus speaking of the marriage relationship, the Savior compares it to the gospel covenant relationship, and the Church. In this covenant relationship, the husband represents Christ, and the wife represents the Church. Ephesians 5:31 says, "For this cause shall a man leave his father and mother, and shall be joined unto his wife, and they two shall be one flesh."

In verse 32 it says, "This is a great mystery: But I speak concerning Christ and the church." Paul is quoting the scripture from Genesis out of context. He is quoting it, and he knows what it means. We know this because he says, "This is a great mystery." A mystery is not something unknowable or spooky. It is sacred knowledge that you can only get if you have been appropriately prepared in a place called the temple.

What this tells me is that Paul knew the doctrine, but he deliberately takes it out of context, "But I speak of Christ and the church." He is using it to make an application, which is fine. Heavenly Mother is also mentioned in Abraham 4:27. This verse is a subtler reference rather than being explicit. There are at least four places in scripture that speak, in my estimation, of a Heavenly Mother.

Let's also look at Genesis 1:26–27. It is amazing to me the rest of the Christian world has these verses of scripture right in front of them and they do not even see a simple, yet vital truth, which we will now discus. In fact, sometimes we, as Latter-day Saints, read these verses and do not comprehend what they say. "And God said, Let us make man in our image, after our likeness: and let them have dominion over the fish of the sea, and over the fowl of the air, and over the cattle, and over all the earth, and over every creeping thing that creepeth upon the earth. So *God created man in his own image*, in the image of God created he him; male and female created he them." In the Hebrew bible the word for God is Elohim.

In Hebrew, the "im" at the end of any word makes it plural. Elohim, that's how you say God in Hebrew. However, the King James translators just simply translated it as *God*. In Abraham 4:27 it reads, "So the Gods went down to organize man in their own image, in the image of the Gods to form they him, male and female to form they them" (emphasis added). It is interesting to notice that in Abraham's account it says, "the Gods." Often when we read the book of Abraham we think that when it says "Gods" it refers to Heavenly Father and Jesus Christ, and that is correct. However, President Kimball said, "God made man in His own image, and certainly he made woman in the image of His wife partner."[68] It could be said that our ultimate destiny is to live eternally in the marriage relationship as future gods and goddesses, or, as Heavenly parents.

Many years ago, I was teaching a Family Home Evening lesson and the topic was centered on the characteristics of our Heavenly Father. The lesson was not only basic in content but simple in delivery as well. My oldest daughter, who was about nine years old at the time, raised her hand to ask a question. "Dad, where did Heavenly Father come from?" I responded that Heavenly Father was an exalted man and that he was once like us, meaning that he was mortal and lived on an earth like ours. I quoted off the top of my head the couplet from Lorenzo Snow that so many Latter-day Saints are fond of referencing: "As man is, God once was, and as God is, man may be." She was speechless, stunned, and thrilled at the same time. Then came her next question: "Dad, does that mean that Heavenly Father had a Heavenly Father?" I replied in the affirmative. "Wait! Dad! Who then was Heavenly Father's Heavenly Father's Heavenly Father? Whoa! . . . DAD, wait . . . who was the first Heavenly Father?" Her mind was ready to burst. It would have been a hilarious moment had it not been such a sincere, poignant, and in-depth moment at the same time. We had just run into (maybe "slammed into" is a better phrase) that philosophical wall that youth and adults often run into when exploring such questions.

The hymn "If You Could Hie to Kolob" begs answer to the question in its first verse: "Can you find out the generation where Gods began to be?"[69] The implied answer in the verses that follow give the baffling, mind numbing, and incomprehensible answer: "There is no end . . ." No

---

68. Spencer W. Kimball, *Teachings of Spencer W. Kimball,* edited by Edward L. Kimball (Salt Lake City: Bookcraft, 1982), 25.
69. "If You Could Hie to Kolob," *Hymns,* no. 284.

end, nor is there a beginning to the cycles of exaltation that have been occurring throughout eternity. Although I quickly ran out of answers with my daughter that night, we ended up having an incredible discussion about some of the fundamental realities of our existence and at the same time explored some of the core doctrines relating to God's plan of salvation. I like to refer to these doctrines as the Four Pillars of Eternity. These doctrines are not only the four core doctrines of God's plan, but they are also the four foundational doctrines of the temple endowment. The endowment is thus a school that teaches us not only about "our" existence, but also the very nature of existence and the reality that comprises all of our lives.

Pillars of Eternity

The term "Pillars of Eternity" is not new. Others have used this term before but usually in the context of just three pillars. Elder Bruce R. McConkie stated, "The three pillars of eternity [are] the three great eternal verities upon which salvation rests." Further, he states that these are "the three greatest events that have ever occurred in all eternity . . . the three events, preeminent and transcendent above all others, [which] are the creation, the fall, and the atonement."[70]

Similarly, President Nelson has said, "As it is central to the plan, we should try to comprehend the meaning of the Atonement. Before we can comprehend it, though, we must understand the fall of Adam. And before we can fully appreciate the Fall, we must first comprehend the Creation. These three events—the Creation, the Fall, and the Atonement—are three preeminent pillars of God's plan, and they are doctrinally interrelated."[71]

Not to upstage any of these afore mentioned voices, I would propose the addition of a "fourth" pillar of eternity, namely, exaltation or Godhood (eternal life would be another synonym). The following chart shows the interrelationship that occurs between these doctrines:

---

70. Bruce R. McConkie, "The Three Pillars of Eternity," devotional, Brigham Young University, Feb. 17, 1981. See speeches.byu.edu; accessed July 30, 2019.

71. Russell M. Nelson, "Constancy amid Change," *Ensign*, Nov. 1993, 33.

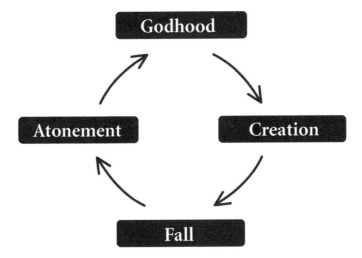

This fourth pillar is not only worth mentioning but also warrants inclusion with the three pillars, because it is the end outcome and desired goal and purpose of the plan of salvation. Without eternal life and exaltation (Godhood), there could be no creation and thus no continuance of this eternal cycle. Indeed, Elder McConkie claims that, "Without any one of them all things would lose their purpose and meaning, and the plans and designs of Deity would come to naught. If there had been no creation, we would not be, neither the earth, nor any form of life upon its face. All things, all the primal elements, would be without form and void. God would have no spirit children; there would be no mortal probation; and none of us would be on the way to *immortality and eternal life*."[72]

Similarly, Elder Boyd K. Packer has stated, "This we know! This simple truth! Had there been no Creation, no Fall, there should have been no need for any Atonement, neither a Redeemer to mediate for us. Then Christ need not have been."[73] In short, God creates things. He sets up conditions whereby things can fall.[74] He provides a way so those things can be redeemed through the Atonement, and all of this so that we can become exalted beings one day like our Father and Mother in

---

72. McConkie, "The Three Pillars of Eternity"; emphasis added.

73. Boyd K. Packer, "Atonement, Agency, Accountability," *Ensign*, May 1988.

74. God cannot create fallen things. He can only set up conditions whereby things can fall through the exercise of agency. Things must become fallen as an eternal principle, since there "must needs be opposition in all things."

heaven—even gods and goddesses. And what do Gods do? They create things—and the cycle continues. This reality is encapsulated so well in the following verses from the Book of Mormon: "My soul delighteth in proving unto my people that save Christ should come all men must perish. For if there be no Christ there be no God; and if there be no God we are not, for there could have been no creation. But there is a God" (2 Nephi 11:6–7).

Another way to say this is if there be no Atonement (no Christ), then there can be no Gods; and if there are no Gods, then things cannot be created. We then are doing (and going through) the same thing that our Heavenly Father went through and that which His Heavenly Father went through. This notion that we are doing "that which is done on other worlds" is central to the theology of the temple. In summary, we are following a grand, eternal pattern, as suggested by Orson Pratt:

> The dealing of God towards his children from the time they are first born in Heaven, through all their successive stages of existence, until they are redeemed, perfected, and made Gods, is a pattern after which all other worlds are dealt with. . . . The creation, fall, and redemption of all future worlds with their inhabitants will be conducted upon the same general plan. . . . The Father of our spirits has only been doing that which His progenitors did before Him. Each succeeding generation of Gods follow the example of the preceding ones. . . . [The same plan of redemption is carried out] by which more ancient worlds have been redeemed. . . . Thus will worlds and systems of worlds . . . be multiplied in endless succession through the infinite depths of boundless space; some telestial, some terrestrial, and some Celestial, differing in their glory.[75]

The diagram on the following page is thus an illustration of this reality, and an amplification of the previous chart in extended version:

75. Orson Pratt, *The Seer*, "Pre-existence" (American Fork, UT: Seagull Book, 1993), 134–35.

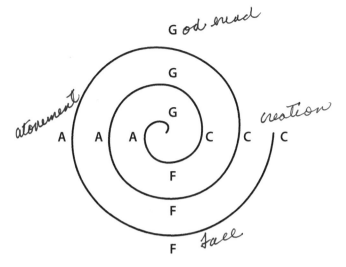

In the holy temple, all teaching centers on and derives itself from these four foundational doctrines. Furthermore we learn therein that this cycle, which produces exaltation and eternal lives (D&C 132) is an unending cycle throughout all eternity. No wonder that in the ordinance of the endowment, the most lengthy time wise of all the saving ordinances, we find each one of these doctrines amply taught, not only in their beautiful, allegorical fulness, but also in an interconnected fashion with the other core doctrines.

It is interesting to note that the prophets in the Book of Mormon taught these same doctrines as well to their listeners: "And it came to pass that when Aaron saw that the king would believe his words, he began from the *creation* of Adam, reading the scriptures unto the king—how *God created man* after his own image, and that God gave him command-ments, and that because of transgression, *man had fallen*. And Aaron did expound unto him the scriptures from the creation of Adam, laying *the fall of man* before him, and their carnal state *and also the plan of redemption*, which was prepared from the foundation of the world, *through Christ*, for all whosoever would believe on his name . . . And it came to pass that after Aaron had expounded these things unto him, the king said: What shall I do that I may have *this eternal life* of which thou hast spoken?" (Alma 22:12–13, 15, emphasis added).

The Fourth Pillar: Exaltation, Eternal Life, and Godhood

At this point, let us say a few words about this final and fourth pillar, namely, exaltation, eternal life, or godhood. All of these afore mentioned terms are actually synonyms and describe a potential goal that both men and women can reach together if they so choose. Other scriptural terms describe this exalted state as well. Those who become exalted, who inherit eternal life, are individuals who also receive "eternal increase" (D&C 131). They receive "all power" and the "continuation of the seeds" (D&C 132). They receive the "father's kingdom" and "all that the Father hath" (D&C 84:33–38). They are filled "with His glory" and are "made equal with Him" (D&C 88:107). They become "joint heirs" with Christ (Romans 8:17), and they "sit in His throne" (Revelation 3:21). In short, they become gods and goddesses.

Although some might consider such status as blasphemous or downright impossible, we learn from the Savior himself that such an attainment is not only possible but also commanded. "Be ye therefore perfect, even as your Father which is in heaven is perfect" (Matthew 5:48). C. S. Lewis's words are memorable:

> Imagine yourself as a living house. God comes in to rebuild that house. At first, perhaps, you can understand what He is doing. He is getting the drains right and stopping the leaks in the roof and so on: you knew that those jobs needed doing and so you are not surprised. But presently He starts knocking the house about in a way that hurts abominably and does not seem to make sense. What on earth is He up to? The explanation is that He is building quite a different house from the one you thought of—throwing out a new wing here, putting on an extra floor there, running up towers, making courtyards. You thought you were going to be made into a decent little cottage: but He is building a palace. The command Be ye perfect is not idealistic gas. Nor is it a command to do the impossible. He is going to make us into creatures that can obey that command. He said (in the Bible) that we were "gods" and He is going to make good His words. If we let Him—for we can prevent Him, if we choose—He will make the feeblest and filthiest of us into a god or goddess, dazzling, radiant, immortal creature, pulsating all through with such energy and joy and wisdom and love as we cannot now imagine. *The process will be long*

and in parts very painful; but that is what we are in for. Nothing less. He meant what He said."[76]

Lewis's words remind us that such a lofty achievement, while certainly possible, is not something that will occur immediately. The first Presidency taught, "Man is the child of God, formed in the divine image and endowed with divine attributes, and even as the infant son of an earthly father and mother is capable in due time of becoming a man, so the undeveloped offspring of celestial parentage is capable, by experience through ages and eons, of evolving into a God."[77]

The Default Position of Salvation and Exaltation

The preceding analogy from the first presidency is intriguing and is worth a closer examination. The question is not whether the infant will develop into a full grown adult or not, that has already been determined. The child is genetically engineered to become such. We are pre-programmed, if you will, to achieve our biological destiny. We are not wondering if the child will become a horse, a fly, or a snake. No, the outcome is certain; it is set. It was foreordained long ago. No amount of wishing, worrying, trying, or not trying will change things.

Similarly, we all, being sons and daughters of Heavenly Parents, are engineered and designed from the beginning to become exalted beings one day. In fact, we have been given exaltation provisionally. The question is not whether we will earn it, but whether we will let go of what we already have. We have the promises; we have the assurance. The default position of salvation and exaltation is not that we don't have it and are trying to get to it, but that we already have it and are here on earth trying to decide if we will finish becoming what we were designed to be. Eternal life isn't a door prize or salary payment. It is a realization or attainment of our divine and eternal potential. Moses realized this truth when he declared to the Lord, "Thou hast made me, and *given unto me a right to thy throne*, and not of myself, *but through thine own grace*" (Moses 7:59, emphasis added).

---

76. C. S. Lewis, *Mere Christianity* (Indianapolis, IN: Collier, 1960), 174; emphasis added.
77. Smith, Winder, and Lund, "The Origin of Man."

What a beautiful truth! We have *a right* to the throne! This is to say that we have a right to exaltation and eternal life. It is indeed our birthright. This is what we were divinely engineered to become. As previously stated, the issue then is not whether we are ever going to do enough to "earn" eternal life. No, that has already been done by the Savior through his "own grace," as the scripture says. Again, the issue is whether we will let go of what we already have.

Similarly in Abraham 3:26 we read, "And they who *keep their first estate* shall be added upon; and they who *keep not their first estate* shall not have glory in the same kingdom with those who *keep their first estate*; and they who *keep their second estate* shall have glory added upon their heads forever and ever."

We do not "earn" our estates, we keep them. In 2 Nephi 2:4 we are told that "the way is prepared from the fall of man, and salvation is free." Salvation in any form (not just physical death) is not something we earn. It has already been given to us. The only issue to decide is if we will hold on to this precious gift and endowment. Such a realization should fill our hearts and minds with unrestrained peace and serenity. It should cause us to worry less and rejoice more. The Lord's teachings on this matter are consistent and sure:

- "Fear not, and be just for *the Kingdom is ours.*"[78]
- "I will be merciful unto you, for *I have given unto you the kingdom*" (D&C 64:4; emphasis added).
- "For *ye are lawful heirs*, according to the flesh, and have been hid from the world with Christ in God" (D&C 86:9; emphasis added).
- "Peace be with you; my blessings continue with you. *For even yet the kingdom is yours, and shall be forever, if you fall not* from your steadfastness" (D&C 82:24; emphasis added).
- "And ye cannot bear all things now; nevertheless, be of good cheer, for I will lead you along. *The kingdom is yours and the blessings thereof are yours, and the riches of eternity are yours*" (D&C 78:18; emphasis added).

---

78. "Redeemer of Israel," *Hymns*, no. 4.

- "And if ye be Christ's, then are ye Abraham's seed, *and heirs according to the promise*" (Galatians 3:29, emphasis added; compare to Romans 9:6).

- "To him that overcometh *will I grant to sit with me in my throne*, even as I also overcame, and am set down with my Father in his throne" (Revelation 3:21).

In Matthew 5:5, we learn that the meek do not earn the earth. They "inherit the earth." (See also Alma 5:51; 3 Nephi 11:38; Alma 5:58; and Alma 40:26.) People do not have to do anything to receive an inheritance (apart from being born into a family with riches—and we have been born into an eternal family with eternal riches). In Mosiah 27:25–26 it says, "And the Lord said unto me: Marvel not that all mankind, yea, men and women, all nations, kindreds, tongues and people, must be born again; yea, born of God, changed from their carnal and fallen state, to a state of righteousness, being redeemed of God, becoming his sons and daughters; and thus they become new creatures; and unless they do this, they can in nowise *inherit the kingdom of God*." It is true that when we inherit something it isn't earned. It is a free gift given. However, even though we don't earn an inheritance, we can, if we are not careful, disinherit ourselves.

With the knowledge that the "promises are yours" (D&C 132:31), we should quit worrying and start living and becoming. They key is to never give up trying . . . because we will get there.

The Lord said to Oliver Granger, "Therefore, let him contend earnestly for the redemption of the First Presidency of my Church, saith the Lord; *and when he falls he shall rise again*, for his sacrifice shall be more sacred unto me than his increase, saith the Lord" (D&C 117:13).

President Boyd K. Packer's commentary on this verse is memorable:

Some worry endlessly over missions that were missed, or marriages that did not turn out, or babies that did not arrive, or children that seem lost, or dreams unfulfilled, or because age limits what they can do. I do not think it pleases the Lord when we worry because we think we never do enough or that what we do is never good enough. Some needlessly carry a heavy burden of guilt which could be removed through confession and repentance. The Lord did not say of Oliver, "[If] he falls," but "When he falls he shall rise again."[79]

---

79. Boyd K. Packer, "The Least of These," *Ensign*, Nov. 2004.

We all make mistakes. We all "fall short of the glory of God" (Romans 3:23). The key is to never give up, to keep rising, because eventually we will get to our eternal destiny if we do not quit.

C.S. Lewis wrote,

We may, indeed, be sure that perfect chastity—like perfect charity—will not be attained by any merely human efforts. You must ask for God's help. Even when you have done so, it may seem to you for a long time that no help, or less help than you need, is being given. Never mind. After each failure, ask forgiveness, pick yourself up, and try again. Very often, what God first helps us toward is not the virtue itself but just this power of always trying again. For however important chastity (or courage, or truthfulness, or any other virtue) may be, this process trains us in habits of the soul which are more important still. It cures our illusions about ourselves and teaches us to depend on God. We learn, on the one hand, that we cannot trust ourselves even in our best moments, and, on the other, that we need not despair even in our worst, for our failures are forgiven. The only fatal thing is to sit down content with anything less than perfection.[80]

Hymns That Include Heavenly Mother

"Oh My Father," *Hymns*, no. 292

> When I leave this frail existence,
> When I lay this mortal by,
> *Father, Mother,* may I meet you
> In your royal courts on high?
> Then, at length, when I've completed
> All you sent me forth to do,
> With your mutual approbation
> Let me come and dwell with you.

"Oh, What Songs of the Heart," *Hymns*, no. 286

> Oh, what songs we'll employ!
> Oh, what welcome we'll hear!

---

80. Lewis, *Mere Christianity*.

While our transports of love are complete,
As the heart swells with joy
In embraces most dear
When our heavenly parents we meet!
As the heart swells with joy,
Oh, what songs we'll employ,
When our heavenly parents we meet!

"We Meet Again as Sisters," *Hymns*, no. 311

We meet to sing together
The praises of our Lord,
To seek our exaltation
According to his word.
To ev'ry gospel blessing
The Lord has turned the key,
That we, *with heav'nly parents*,
May sing eternally.

The women of this dispensation are distinct from the women of any other . . . this distinction brings both privileges and responsibilities. . . . dear sisters . . . we, your brethren, need your strength, your conversion, your conviction, your ability to lead, your wisdom, and your voices. The kingdom of God is not and cannot be complete without women who make sacred covenants and then keep them, women who can speak with the power and authority of God!

—President Russell M. Nelson
"A Plea to My Sisters," *Ensign*, October 2015

Part 2

EQUALITY, GENDER ROLES, AND BALANCE

Chapter 5

Equality, Gender Roles, and Presiding in Righteousness

Of all the creations of the Almighty, there is none more beautiful, none more inspiring than a lovely daughter of God who walks in virtue with an understanding of why she should do so, who honors and respects her body as a thing sacred and divine, who cultivates her mind and constantly enlarges the horizon of her understanding, who nurtures her spirit with everlasting truth.[81]

—President Gordon B. Hinckley

Years ago, a humorous story was shared in conference by President Boyd K. Packer to illustrate a gospel principle relating to gender differences. The principle he was teaching touches on something that has become a huge social issue in recent years, and even carries serious moral overtones that have caused some to question the legitimacy and need for religious voices. He was supervising Church education programs and was on a visit to a church school in Albuquerque when the principal told him of an incident that occurred in a first-grade class.

---

81. Gordon B. Hinckley, "Our Responsibility to Our Young Women," *Ensign*, Sept. 1988.

During a lesson, a kitten wandered into the room and distracted the youngsters. It was brought to the front of the room so all could see it. One youngster asked,

"Is it a boy kitty or a girl kitty?"

The teacher, unprepared for that discussion, said, "It doesn't matter; it's just a kitten."

But the children persisted, and one little boy said, "I know how we can tell if it is a boy kitty or a girl kitty."

The teacher, cornered, said, "All right, you tell us how we can tell if it is a boy kitty or a girl kitty."

The boy answered, "We can vote on it!"[82]

President Packer went on to say, "Some things cannot be changed. Doctrine cannot be changed."

President Wilford Woodruff said,

> Principles which have been revealed for the salvation and exaltation of the children of men . . . are principles you cannot annihilate. They are principles that no combination of men [or women] can destroy. They are principles that can never die. . . . They are beyond the reach of man to handle or to destroy. . . . It is not in the power of the whole world put together to destroy those principles. . . . Not one jot or tittle of these principles will ever be destroyed.[83]

We live in an interesting day and age in which a variety of social, political, and legal voices are demanding actions and changes that often blur the lines of gender, identity, and associated roles and expectations. While there have been many positive changes in the way we administer justice and secure the rights and protections of all people, there seems to be at times an escalating surge of unrestrained philosophies and practices which potentially threaten other inherent freedoms and strike at the foundation of the well-being of society. Gospel truths and fundamental laws of nature are often derided and discarded in favor of capricious notions which all too often tear down families and make a mockery of God's eternal laws.

One of these specific changes that has occurred in recent years is the way in which we view the ideal of *equality*, especially as it relates to gender

82. Packer, "For Time and All Eternity."
83. Wilford Woodruff in *Journal of Discourses*, 22:342.

roles. While many of the changes in this area are good, it is important to note that there can, and has been, some excesses in the way these changes are facilitated. Thoughtful scholars have noted,

> The restored gospel of Jesus Christ proclaims the doctrine of *equal partnership between men and women*, here and in the eternities. In this context, *it is important to understand what Latter-day Saints mean by the term equal partnership. Equality is all too often mistaken to mean that if two things are equal, they must be identical to each other.*[84]

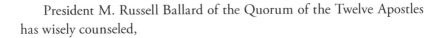

President M. Russell Ballard of the Quorum of the Twelve Apostles has wisely counseled,

> Men and women, *though spiritually equal*, are entrusted with *different but equally significant* roles. . . . Men are given stewardship over the sacred ordinances of the priesthood. To women, God gives stewardship over bestowing and nurturing mortal life, including providing physical bodies for God's spirit children and guiding those children toward a knowledge of gospel truths. These stewardships, *equally sacred and important*, do not involve any false ideas about domination or subordination.[85]

To be sure, equality is not only an important social topic, it is an eternal gospel principle. "That you may be equal in the bonds of heavenly things, yea, and earthly things also. . . . For if ye are not equal in earthly things ye cannot be equal in obtaining heavenly things" (D&C 78:5–6; see also D&C 82:17–19). Also, "Nevertheless, in your temporal things you shall be equal, and this not grudgingly, otherwise the abundance of the manifestations of the Spirit shall be withheld" (D&C 70:14).

Prophetic Voices Call for Equality

In recent years, living prophets have extolled the virtue of equality in marriage and have sought to properly define its limits while adamantly ensuring its necessary existence. One notable teaching was given in a

84. Valerie M. Hudson and Richard B. Miller, "Equal Partnership in Marriage," *Ensign*, April 2013; emphasis added.
85. M. Russell Ballard, "The Sacred Responsibilities of Parenthood," *Ensign*, Mar. 2006, 29–30; emphasis added.

priesthood session of general conference by then President Howard W. Hunter:

> A man . . . *accepts his wife as a partner in the leadership of the home and family* with *full knowledge* of and *full participation in all decisions* relating thereto. . . . The Lord intended that the wife be . . . *a companion equal and necessary in full partnership.* Presiding in righteousness necessitates a *shared responsibility between husband and wife;* together you act with knowledge and participation in all family matters. For a man to operate independent of or without regard to the feelings and counsel of his wife . . . is to exercise unrighteous dominion.[86]

In similar fashion, President Boyd K. Packer has taught, "In the Church there is a distinct line of authority. We serve where called by those who preside over us. *In the home it is a partnership with husband and wife equally yoked together, sharing in decisions, always working together.*"[87]

Elder L. Tom Perry of the Quorum of the Twelve Apostles has also counseled, "There is not a president or a vice president in a family. The couple *works together* . . . They are on *equal footing.* They plan and organize the affairs of the family *jointly and unanimously* as they move forward."[88]

Recently, President Henry B. Eyring has spoken of the extremely important role that both men and women have with respect to gospel education in the home, especially with the advent of the "home-centered, Church-supported" model inherent in the new two-hour approach to Sunday worship services. His words not only highlight the important place of women in this effort, but he also suggests that it is women, not men, who should fulfill the role of principal gospel educator in the family. He taught,

> You might ask, "How does that make faithful sisters a primary force to help the Lord pour out knowledge on His Saints?" The Lord gives the answer in "The Family: A Proclamation to the World." You remember the words, but you may see new meaning and recognize that the Lord foresaw these exciting changes, which are now occurring. In the proclamation, *He gave sisters charge to be the principal gospel educators*

---

86. Howard W. Hunter, "Being a Righteous Husband and Father," *Ensign,* Nov. 1994; emphasis added.

87. Boyd K. Packer, "The Relief Society," *Ensign,* May 1998, 73.

88. L. Tom Perry, "Fatherhood, an Eternal Calling," *Ensign,* May 2004, 71.

in the family in these words: "Mothers are primarily responsible for the nurture of their children." This includes the nurture of gospel truth and knowledge. Why, then, does a daughter of God in a united and equal relationship *receive the primary responsibility to nourish with the most important nutrient all must receive, a knowledge of truth coming from heaven*? As nearly as I can see, that has been the Lord's way since families were created in this world. For instance, it was Eve who received the knowledge that Adam needed to partake of the fruit of the tree of knowledge for them to keep all of God's commandments and to form a family. I do not know why it came to Eve first, but Adam and Eve were perfectly united when the knowledge was poured out on Adam.[89]

Story of a Nurturing Mother

My mother was an excellent and natural example of this type of gospel leading and teaching. I'll never forget one experience that occurred many years ago when our family lived in Denver, Colorado. I was nine or ten years old at the time and had just recently come home from a Cub Scout meeting. I had just gone downstairs to my basement bedroom and had proceeded to sit on my bed, which was directly under part of the false, drop ceiling that covered some of the heating ducts. As I recall, it was a somewhat older home, and the finish work in the basement was slightly less than professional grade.

As I was sitting on my bed, I started to unbutton my blue Cub Scout shirt, when I suddenly heard an almost audible voice: "Get up and move." It was very distinct, yet strange—so strange and odd that I ignored it and continued to unbutton my shirt. I got about half way through the buttons when the voice came a second time with the exact same message: "Get up and move!" This time I was shocked, because it seemed almost audible. I even thought for a moment that one of my brothers might be whispering something from behind their beds, perhaps teasing me. Well, I ignored the voice again and continued to unbutton the rest of my shirt. Suddenly, the voice came for the third time: "Get up and move—NOW!" It was strong, distinct, and incredibly urgent. I was startled and immediately stood up and walked away from the bed. I'd moved about three or four steps away when almost instinctively, as it were, I stopped, turned around, and faced my bed. To this day, I still cannot believe what happened next.

---

89. Henry B. Eyring, "Women and Gospel Learning in the Home," *Ensign*, Nov. 2018.

The moment I turned around, an eight-by-five-foot section of the false ceiling—sheetrock, ceiling tiles, nails, two-by-fours—came crashing down in one quick, loud thump on my bed. Sheetrock dust was billowing upward and filling the room.

Almost immediately, a piercing voice came from upstairs: "Charles Robert! What have you done?!" Footsteps were now racing down the stairs—it was my mother! I was in a panic. I needed to hide the mess . . . but how? I stood motionless as she came bolting into the bedroom.

"What happened?" she asked. "Are you okay?"

In shock, I told her I was fine, but it was a good thing I had moved so quickly off my bed.

She said, "You were on your bed?"

I told her yes, I was, but it was good I had followed the voice that had spoken to me.

She was concerned and a bit confused. "You heard a voice?"

I answered, "Yes, I did—well, actually I didn't listen to it the first three times, but I got scared and finally moved." I still did not get what was going on.

It took my dad, my brothers, and me—all of us—to move the piece of ceiling off my bed later that night. I still remember Dad telling me that had I not moved, it probably would have snapped my neck in half.

What I remember most about this amazing experience wasn't so much the miraculous nature of hearing the heavenly voice of warning. No, it was the comforting, loving, and instructing voice of my mother later that night as she spoke with me about the Holy Ghost, the Spirit, and the still, small voice. She expressed to me that I for sure had someone watching out for me on the other side of the veil and that I was preserved for a reason. The spirit of her love, nurturing, and counsel can still be felt in my heart all these years later, and I will be forever grateful for the way she so naturally and lovingly taught the gospel in our home.

It has been said that

> Motherhood [is] a holy calling, a sacred dedication for carrying out the Lord's plans, a consecration of devotion to the upbringing and fostering, the nurturing in body, mind, and spirit, of those who kept their first estate and who come to this earth for their second estate. This divine service of motherhood can be rendered only by mothers. It may not be passed to others. Nurses cannot do it; public nurseries cannot do it; hired help cannot do it—only mother, aided as much as may be

by the loving hands of father, brothers, and sisters, can give the full needed measure of watchful care. Motherhood is near to divinity. It is the highest, holiest service to be assumed by mankind. It places her who honors its holy calling and service next to the angels.[90]

Analogy of the Tree

Some years ago, Elder F. Enzio Busche gave this wise counsel about gender roles and the type of equality that can and should exist between husband and wife:

> The priesthood is neither male nor female, although it has a male part and a female part. Through the eternal bond of marriage, built on the divine gift of love, the priesthood becomes complete. The roles of the two parts are, of course, vastly different. Heavenly Father has given the female the role of bringing new life to this world. She does so in a physical dimension—by nurturing, tutoring, training, and teaching—and in the wearing of the very eternal virtues of chastity, loyalty, and wholesomeness, which are essential for the very existence of humankind. Our Heavenly Father has given the male the role of providing, protecting, and admiring. Male and female are in many ways mysteriously different and, because of that, there is a natural desire to love one another in harmony with the divine laws as they have been reestablished by the restoration of the gospel.[91]

He then shares a wonderful analogy to explain these differences and unity:

> The best way to gain an understanding of the male and female part of the priesthood is to be reminded of a tree. As we look at a tree, it appears to be complete with its trunk, branches, leaves, and blossoms; but we know that another, equally important part of the tree [exists]. The roots—[sometimes] unseen, lie deeply embedded in the soil— are constantly nourishing and strengthening the visible parts of the tree. The roots do not argue with the trunk. They both enjoy oneness.

90. J. Reuben Clark, "Parenthood," Message of the First Presidency, in Conference Report, Oct. 1942, 7, 11–12.

91. F. Enzio Busche, *Yearning for the Living God* (Salt Lake City: Deseret Book, 2004), 215.

The temple is the Lord's essential instrument used to reestablish a true understanding of the male and female parts of the priesthood.[92]

He concludes by reminding us that

No man can excel in his priesthood calling for long without the blessing and care and guidance of a righteous woman. When we listen carefully in the temple and learn to understand and accept our male and female roles, we will soon see ourselves in our own limitations. Those who concentrate their efforts in developing the purposes and virtues of their own gender will build tender, bonding bridges between men and women on the basis of mutual respect and admiration . . . A society that fails to accept the eternal concept of this godly design must pay an unbearable price of confusion of the individual, which can potentially lead to chaos, destruction, and the unhappiness of the soul.[93]

Women Working Outside of the Home

During my career as a BYU religion instructor and Church religious education teacher, I have come to appreciate many other statements from Church leaders with regard to gender roles of both men and women. Speaking of the issue of women working outside of the home, President Gordon B. Hinckley counseled,

Some years ago, President Benson delivered a message to the women of the Church. He encouraged them to leave their employment and give their individual time to their children. I sustain the position he took. Nevertheless, I recognize, as he recognized, that there are some women (it has become very many in fact) who have to work to provide for the needs of their families. To you I say, do the very best you can. I hope that if you are employed full-time you are doing it to ensure that *basic needs* are met and not simply to indulge a taste for an elaborate home, fancy cars, and other luxuries. The greatest job that any mother will ever do will be in nurturing, teaching, lifting, encouraging, and rearing her children in righteousness and truth. None other can adequately take her place. It is well-nigh impossible to be a full-time homemaker and a full-time employee. I know how some of you struggle with decisions concerning this matter. I repeat, do the very best you can. You know

92. Ibid.
93. Ibid.

64

your circumstances, and I know that you are deeply concerned for the welfare of your children. Each of you has a bishop who will counsel with you and assist you. To the mothers of this Church, every mother who is here today, I want to say that as the years pass, you will become increasingly grateful for that which you did in molding the lives of your children in the direction of righteousness and goodness, integrity and faith. That is most likely to happen if you can spend adequate time with them.[94]

Other prophets through the years have also emphasized the importance of the home. President David O. McKay's words are memorable and timeless: "No other success can compensate for failure in the home."[95]

Similarly, President Harold B. Lee counseled, "The most important of the Lord's work that you [fathers] will ever do will be the work you do within the walls of your own home."[96]

Though President Hinckley has qualified these teachings, as discussed previously, it is helpful to remember not only the words, but also the spirit of President Benson's counsel:

In a home where there is an able-bodied husband, he is expected to be the breadwinner. Sometimes we hear of husbands who, because of economic conditions, have lost their jobs and expect the wives to go out of the home and work, even though the husband is still capable of providing for his family. In these cases, we urge the husband to do all in his power to allow his wife to remain in the home caring for the children while he continues to provide for his family the best he can, even though the job he is able to secure may not be ideal and family budgeting may have to be tighter. Brethren of the priesthood, I continue to emphasize the importance of mothers staying home to nurture, care for, and train their children in the principles of righteousness. As I travel throughout the Church, I feel that the great majority of Latter-day Saint mothers earnestly want to follow this counsel. But we know that sometimes the mother works outside of the home at the encouragement, or even insistence, of her husband. It is he who wants the items of convenience that the extra income can buy. Not only will the family suffer in such instances, brethren, but *your own spiritual growth and progression will*

94. Gordon B. Hinckley, "Women of the Church," *Ensign*, Nov. 1996.
95. David O. McKay, "Home Building Paramount," in Conference Report, Apr. 1935, 116. This was the first time David O. McKay gave this counsel.
96. President Harold B. Lee, *Strengthening the Home* (pamphlet), 1973, 7.

be hampered. I say to all of you, the Lord has charged men with the responsibility to provide for their families in such a way that the wife is allowed to fulfill her role as mother in the home.[97]

President Henry B. Eyring has also offered the following summary of many of the important points of prophetic counsel on this particular topic:

In our own time, we have been warned with counsel of where to find safety from sin and from sorrow. One of the keys to recognizing those warnings is that they are repeated. For instance, more than once in these general conferences, you have heard our prophet say that he would quote a preceding prophet and would therefore be a second witness and sometimes even a third. Each of us who has listened has heard President Kimball give counsel on the importance of a mother in the home and then heard President Benson quote him, and we have heard President Hinckley quote them both. The Apostle Paul wrote that in the mouth of two or three witnesses shall every word be established. One of the ways we may know that the warning is from the Lord is that the law of witnesses, authorized witnesses, has been invoked. When the words of prophets seem repetitive, that should rivet our attention and fill our hearts with gratitude to live in such a blessed time.[98]

Finally, President Boyd K. Packer's counsel is likewise memorable and worthy of inclusion along with the previous prophetic voice we have cited:

Except Adam and Eve by nature be different from one another, they could not multiply and fill the earth. The complementing differences are the very key to the plan of happiness. Some roles are best suited to the masculine nature and others to the feminine nature. Both the scriptures and the patterns of nature place man as the protector, the provider. Those responsibilities of the priesthood, which have to do with the administration of the Church, of necessity function outside the home. By divine decree, they have been entrusted to men. It has been that way since the beginning. A man who holds the priesthood does not have an advantage over a woman in qualifying for exaltation. The woman, by her very nature, is also cocreator with God and the primary nurturer of the children. Virtues and attributes upon which

---

97. Ezra Taft Benson, "To the Fathers in Israel," *Ensign*, Nov. 1987, 51.

98. Henry B. Eyring, "Finding Safety in Counsel," *Ensign*, May 1997, 25.

perfection and exaltation depend come naturally to a woman and are refined through marriage and motherhood. The priesthood is conferred only upon worthy men in order to conform to our Father's plan of happiness. With the laws of nature and the revealed word of God working in harmony, it simply works best that way. Natural and spiritual laws which govern life were instituted from before the foundation of the world. They are eternal, as are the consequences for either obeying or disobeying them. They are not based on social or political considerations. They cannot be changed. No pressure, no protest, no legislation can alter them.[99]

On another occasion President Packer said,

Our Father's plan requires that, like the generation of life itself, the shield of faith is to be made and fitted in the family. No two can be exactly alike. Each must be handcrafted to individual specifications. The plan designed by the Father contemplates that man and woman, husband and wife, working together, fit each child individually with a shield of faith made to buckle on so firmly that it can neither be pulled off nor penetrated by those fiery darts. It takes the steady strength of a father to hammer out the metal of it and the tender hands of a mother to polish and fit it on. Sometimes one parent is left to do it alone. It is difficult, but it can be done. In the Church we can teach about the materials from which a shield of faith is made: reverence, courage, chastity, repentance, forgiveness, compassion. In church we can learn how to assemble and fit them together. But the actual making of and fitting on of the shield of faith belongs in the family circle. Otherwise it may loosen and come off in a crisis. *This shield of faith is not manufactured on an assembly line, only handmade in a cottage industry.* Therefore our leaders press members to understand that what is most worth doing must be done at home. Some still do not see that too many out-of-home activities, however well intended, leave too little time to make and fit on the shield of faith at home.[100]

99. Packer, "For Time and All Eternity," 22.
100. Boyd K. Packer, "The Shield of Faith," *Ensign*, May 1995.

Chapter 6

Laborers in the Vineyard: A Parable to Understand Equality in God's Plan

*I*n this chapter, we seek to deepen our understanding of the principle of equality in God's eternal plan of salvation. Often when discussions arise about fairness and equality, especially as it relates to gender differences, frustrations, pains, and misconceptions can arise if issues are not correctly viewed through the lens of this plan. Several years ago, I had an intriguing conversation with a good friend regarding the parable of the laborers in the vineyard. This individual was a well-respected leader in the community and very conversant with the restored gospel. He was a hard-working, no-nonsense type who was a self-made man with a somewhat austere and confident character. To his credit, he tried the best he could to live all facets of the gospel with exactness. Indeed, I have never encountered his equal.

We just happened to be talking one day about the gospel and associated symbolism that we sometimes encounter in the scriptures and in the temples. The topic of parables by chance came up. It just so happened at the time of this conversation I had just finished a semester of teaching an institute of religion course entitled "The Parables of Jesus," so naturally I was excited to discuss the topic with him. Out of the blue, he asked, "What is your favorite parable?" That was an easy answer. Although I love many parables, the one for me that had been the most stimulating, the most rewarding to study, was the parable of the laborers in the vineyard.

His countenance dropped when I told him this, and a look of consternation came over him. It was as if I had just committed some horrible crime. Although he was a friend—a close one at that—you would have never known it at that moment. He gazed at me with a piercing stare and simply exclaimed, "You have got to be kidding me. Are you serious?"

I replied, "I am serious. It is my favorite parable."

His reply: "I hate that parable!"

I could tell that he was sincere with his feelings and that he meant what he said. I asked him why he did not like the parable. With a tone of repugnance, he declared, "It's just not fair!"

The Parable

> For the kingdom of heaven is like unto a man that is an householder, which went out early in the morning to hire labourers into his vineyard. And when he had agreed with the labourers for a penny a day, he sent them into his vineyard. And he went out about the third hour, and saw others standing idle in the marketplace, And said unto them; Go ye also into the vineyard, and whatsoever is right I will give you. And they went their way. Again he went out about the sixth and ninth hour, and did likewise. And about the eleventh hour he went out, and found others standing idle, and saith unto them, Why stand ye here all the day idle? They say unto him, Because no man hath hired us. He saith unto them, Go ye also into the vineyard; and whatsoever is right, that shall ye receive. So when even was come, the lord of the vineyard saith unto his steward, Call the labourers, and give them their hire, beginning from the last unto the first. And when they came that were hired about the eleventh hour, they received every man a penny. But when the first came, they supposed that they should have received more; and they likewise received every man a penny. And when they had received it, they murmured against the goodman of the house, Saying, These last have wrought but one hour, and thou hast made them equal unto us, which have borne the burden and heat of the day. But he answered one of them, and said, Friend, I do thee no wrong: didst not thou agree with me for a penny? Take that thine is, and go thy way: I will give unto this last, even as unto thee. Is it not lawful for me to do what I will with mine own? Is thine eye evil, because I am good? So the last shall be first, and the first last: for many be called, but few chosen. (Matthew 20:1–16)

I have thought about the possible reasons why my good friend—or anyone else for that matter—would react so negatively to this parable, and I have concluded that they probably do not understand the symbolic nature of parables.

The Purpose of Parables

Unlike most stories, which are simply that—stories—the Savior used parables to teach in-depth matters regarding himself, his gospel, and more important, his atoning sacrifice for mankind. These matters were so light intensive that He had to exercise caution in teaching. His disciples once asked the Savior why he taught in parables. His reply was instructive: "It is given unto you to know the mysteries of the kingdom of heaven, but to them it is not given. *For* whosoever hath, to him shall be *given*, and he shall have more *abundance*: but whosoever hath not, from him shall be taken away even that he hath. Therefore speak I to them in parables: because they seeing see not; and hearing they hear not, neither do they understand" (Matthew 13:10–13).

Bruce R. McConkie explained it this way:

> Our Lord used parables on frequent occasions during His ministry to teach gospel truths. His purpose, however, in telling these short stories was not to present the truths of His gospel in plainness so that all His hearers would understand. Rather, it was so to phrase and hide the doctrine involved that only the spiritually literate would understand it, while those whose understandings were darkened would remain in darkness. . . . It is never proper to teach any person more than his spiritual capacity qualifies him to assimilate.[101]

The Parable of the Laborers in the Vineyard is indeed a simple story, but much doctrine lies beneath the surface. Those who see this parable as only a story about coins and investments might be prone to derive an interpretation based solely on a monetary mindset. When seen this way, the parable is indeed unfair. But this is not about economics. This parable is about the Lord Jesus Christ and His gospel.

---

101. McConkie, *Mormon Doctrine.*

Interpreting Parables

It can be difficult at times to figure out the true meaning of a parable. Joseph Smith gave a key to correct interpretation: "What is the rule of interpretation? Just no interpretation at all. Understand it precisely as it reads. I have a key by which I understand the scriptures. I enquire, what was the question which drew out the answer, or caused Jesus to utter the parable? To ascertain its meaning, we must dig up the root and ascertain what it was that drew the saying out of Jesus."

Most parables are easier to be understood once their context is understood. To do this with the parable of the laborers in the vineyard, it is necessary to go to Matthew 19, the chapter that precedes the parable found in Matthew 20:

> And, behold, one came and said unto him, Good Master, what good thing shall I do, that I may have eternal life? And he said unto him, Why callest thou me good? there is none good but one, that is, God: but if thou wilt enter into life, keep the commandments. He saith unto him, Which? Jesus said, Thou shalt do no murder, Thou shalt not commit adultery, Thou shalt not steal, Thou shalt not bear false witness, Honour thy father and thy mother: and, Thou shalt love thy neighbour as thyself. The young man saith unto him, All these things have I kept from my youth up: what lack I yet? Jesus said unto him, If thou wilt be perfect, go and sell that thou hast, and give to the poor, and thou shalt have treasure in heaven: and come and follow me. But when the young man heard that saying, he went away sorrowful: for he had great possessions. Then said Jesus unto his disciples, Verily I say unto you, That a rich man shall hardly enter into the kingdom of heaven. And again I say unto you, It is easier for a camel to go through the eye of a needle, than for a rich man to enter into the kingdom of God. When his disciples heard it, they were exceedingly amazed, saying, Who then can be saved? But Jesus beheld them, and said unto them, With men this is impossible; but with God all things are possible. Then answered Peter and said unto him, Behold, we have forsaken all, and followed thee; what shall we have therefore? And Jesus said unto them, Verily I say unto you, That ye which have followed me, in the regeneration when the Son of man shall sit in the throne of his glory, ye also shall sit upon twelve thrones, judging the twelve tribes of Israel. And every one that hath forsaken houses, or brethren, or sisters, or father, or mother, or wife, or children, or lands, for my name's sake, shall receive an

hundredfold, and shall inherit everlasting life. But many that are first shall be last; and the last shall be first. (Matthew 19:16–30)

These verses supply the context to understand the parable. It is interesting to note that Peter is the person whose response provides the impetus for the parable. Usually we think of the Savior directing his reprimands toward the Pharisees and Scribes. Such is not the case in this instance. Elder McConkie explains,

> This difficult parable is closely linked with what goes before, and can only be understood in connection with it. It rebukes the spirit of Peter's enquiry, "We have left all and followed thee; what shall we have?" The Twelve through Peter had demanded a superlatively great reward, because they had been called first and had labored longest. Such a reward had been promised them, should they prove worthy of it, though at the same time it was darkly hinted, that some outside the apostolic circle would prove in the end more worthy than some of the apostles.[102]

The irony of Peter's request is unmistakable: "We have given up everything, so what's in it for us?" The thought is almost comical. It could be said that the parable of the laborers in the vineyard is not just rebuking Peter, but anyone with an overblown sense of entitlement as well. Still, there is more to this parable. The perplexing question raised with regard to the seeming inequality of the rewards given for the work accomplished still demands explanation.

The Righteousness of the Reward

It is interesting to note the way in which the Lord of the Vineyard characterizes the reward. He speaks of it as not only being "right," but also even "lawful." That is to say, the reward is fair and does not violate spiritual law, or the law of justice. The friend I mentioned at the outset might resort to the notion that "mercy cannot rob justice." The fact that the reward is described as being "lawful" would thus mean that mercy is not compromising justice in any way. So then, in what ways is the reward "right" and "lawful?"

---

102. Bruce R. McConkie, *Doctrinal New Testament Commentary*, 3 vols. (Salt Lake City: Bookcraft, 1965–73), 1:560–61.

First of all, everyone agreed on this. Each laborer knew what they would get for the work that would be accomplished. This should be reason enough. But the real reason the reward is just (and here is where we get to the heart of the parable) is that this profound teaching deals with the very essence of the grace and mercy of the Savior's Atonement. Surely we can understand to some extent the complaint of those who labored longest in the vineyard if we see it with the perspective of capitalism. That is to say, we reap what we sow. Not only do the scriptures sustain this notion, but also many philosophies and fiscal sound bites, such as "We get what we work for." "Waste not, want not." "An honest day's wage," and so on. But the interpretation of this parable is neither one that seeks to teach capitalism or any aspect of economic endeavor. This parable is teaching us about the grace and mercy of Jesus Christ.

The Penny and Eternal Life

To fully understand this parable in Matthew 20, it is helpful to go back to the context in Matthew 19. Let us examine the wording more specifically.

> Then said Jesus unto his disciples, Verily I say unto you, That a rich man shall hardly enter into the kingdom of heaven. And again I say unto you, It is easier for a camel to go through the eye of a needle, than for a rich man to enter into the kingdom of God. When his disciples heard it, they were exceedingly amazed, saying, *Who then can be saved?* But Jesus beheld them, and said unto them, *With men this is impossible; but with God all things are possible.* (Matthew 19:23–26, emphasis added)

The question, "who can be saved?" is extremely important. Remember Joseph Smith's rule for interpreting parables: "What was the question which drew out the answer, or caused Jesus to utter the parable?" The answer to the question is sound and doctrinally pure: "with men this is impossible; but with God all things are possible." In other words, we do not save ourselves. Only God can do this. Elder Quentin L. Cook has taught, "We must always remember that we do not save ourselves. We are liberated by the love, grace, and atoning sacrifice of the Savior."[103]

103. Quentin L. Cook, "Lamentations of Jeremiah: Beware of Bondage," *Ensign*, Nov. 2013.

Similarly, Elder Robert D. Hales said, "What does it mean to be a Christian? . . . A Christian believes *that through the grace of God* the Father and His Son, Jesus Christ, *we can repent, forgive others, keep the commandments,* and inherit eternal life."[104]

Elder Uchtdorf's words are also worth noting: "Salvation cannot be bought with the currency of obedience; it is purchased by the blood of the Son of God. . . . Why then obey? . . . our obedience to God's commandments comes as a natural outgrowth of our endless love and gratitude for the goodness of God."[105]

The reward for laboring in the vineyard is not due to our efforts alone. The penny, which symbolizes eternal life, is something none of us can earn. We are told in the scriptures that it is by grace we are saved, after all we can do (2 Nephi 25:23). We are to rely wholly, not partially, upon the merits of Christ (2 Nephi 31:19). In this light, it is ridiculous to think that a certain amount of labor or works (personal righteousness) will satisfy the total price of eternal life.

In this regard, Dallin H. Oaks taught, "Man unquestionably has impressive powers and can bring to pass great things by tireless efforts and an indomitable will. But after all our obedience and good works, we cannot be saved from the effect of our sins without the grace extended by the Atonement of Jesus Christ."[106]

Bruce R. McConkie observed,

Suppose we have the scriptures, the gospel, the priesthood, the Church, the ordinances, the organization, even the keys of the kingdom— everything that now is, down to the last jot and tittle—and yet there is no Atonement of Christ. What then? Can we be saved? Will all our good works save us? Will we be rewarded for all our righteousness? Most assuredly we will not. We are not saved by works alone, no matter how good; we are saved because God sent his Son to shed his blood in Gethsemane and on Calvary that all through him might ransomed be. We are saved by the blood of Christ. To paraphrase Abinadi: Salvation doth not come by the Church alone; and were it not for the Atonement,

---

104. Robert D. Hales, "Being a More Christian Christian," *Ensign*, Nov. 2012.

105. Dieter F. Uchtdorf, "The Gift of Grace," *Ensign*, May 2015.

106. Dallin H. Oaks, "What Think Ye of Christ?" *Ensign*, Nov. 1988, 67.

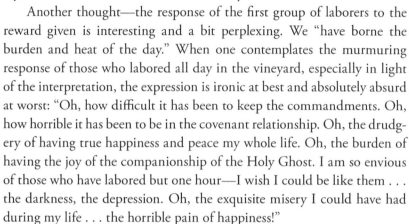

given by the grace of God as a free gift, all men must unavoidably perish, and this notwithstanding the Church and all that appertains to it.[107]

None of us will ever really "earn" or deserve the "penny." That is to say, no mortal will ever merit eternal life by his or her works alone.

Another thought—the response of the first group of laborers to the reward given is interesting and a bit perplexing. We "have borne the burden and heat of the day." When one contemplates the murmuring response of those who labored all day in the vineyard, especially in light of the interpretation, the expression is ironic at best and absolutely absurd at worst: "Oh, how difficult it has been to keep the commandments. Oh, how horrible it has been to be in the covenant relationship. Oh, the drudgery of having true happiness and peace my whole life. Oh, the burden of having the joy of the companionship of the Holy Ghost. I am so envious of those who have labored but one hour—I wish I could be like them . . . the darkness, the depression. Oh, the exquisite misery I could have had during my life . . . the horrible pain of happiness!"

One would expect that the lifetime enjoyment of peace and spiritual prosperity would be in and of itself its own reward, regardless of even greater rewards in the next life. Indeed, the labor we put forth in the gospel is more than just mere work—living the gospel is a way of life. The gospel is a lifestyle that carries its own recompense. One should be delighted to be a laborer in the Lord's vineyard.

When we truly contemplate this antagonistic attitude toward a righteous life, we are almost inclined to ask if the dreary "all-day-long" laborer was truly converted in the first place. Was he just going through the motions? Was his service and commitment to the kingdom for reasons other than those approved by Father in Heaven? Perhaps there are those who labor in the vineyard with a chip on their shoulders, as if they are doing the heavens some great favor. It is as though commitment to the Kingdom is, in their minds, inextricably linked to a life of oppression, frowns, and loathing due to the arduous walk of Christlike living.

Harry Emerson Fosdick perceptively observed,

Some Christians carry their religion on their backs. It is a packet of beliefs and practices which they must bear. At times it grows heavy and

107. Bruce R. McConkie, *The Sermons and Writings of Bruce R. McConkie* (Salt Lake City: Bookcraft, 1989), 76.

they would willingly lay it down, but that would mean a break with old traditions, so they shoulder it again. But real Christians do not carry their religion, their religion carries them. It is not weight; it is wings. It lifts them up, it sees them over hard places, it makes the universe seem friendly, life purposeful, hope real, sacrifice worthwhile. It sets them free from fear, futility, discouragement, and sin—the great enslavers of men's souls. You can know a real Christian, when you see him, by his buoyancy.[108]

The Idle Laborers

Considering the fact that the penny represents the celestial glory of eternal life, these murmuring types and their associated companions (who endure, complain, and despise the life of service) might be shocked to realize that they might not, in the end, even want the reward for which they labored so zealously. "Service is not something we endure on this earth so we can earn the right to live in the celestial kingdom," said President Marion G. Romney. "Service is the very fiber of which an exalted life in the celestial kingdom is made."[109]

Perhaps the focus and attention of these disgruntled laborers is unduly placed on the late-arriving laborers who seemingly "slide" into heaven with no effort. Two thoughts are worth noting in this regard. First, these late arriving types, whom we are told stood "idle" in the market place, are not idle in the sense of being lazy, complacent, or even rebellious. When asked why they were idle, these workers responded by saying, "Because no man hath hired us." It is apparent from this phrase that these workers were in the marketplace and wanted to be hired. They were willing to work, but no work was available at the time. Nevertheless, they waited— diligently, patiently—for work, no matter how much or how little. They did not go home or to the pool hall to pass the time.

Surely, these types should be credited for enduring the uncertainty of unemployment and displaying unwavering vigilance. Surely, their long-working counterparts should respect them for their fortitude and be grateful in the first place that they themselves were afforded the blessed opportunity to be employed all day long. Anyone with experience in real

108. Harry Emerson Fosdick, *Twelve Tests of Character* (1923), 87–88; as quoted in L. Tom Perry's "A Year of Jubilee," *Ensign*, Nov. 1999, 77.

109. Marion G. Romney, "The Celestial Nature of Self-Reliance," *Ensign*, Nov. 1982, 93.

living knows the horrible monotony and depressing curse of not being "anxiously engaged in a good cause." Work is not drudgery, but the lack thereof might be.

J. Richard Clarke quoted the following in the welfare session of the April 1982 general conference:

> If you are poor, work. . . . If you are happy, work. Idleness gives room for doubts and fears. If disappointments come, keep right on working. If sorrow overwhelms you, . . . work. . . . When faith falters and reason fails, just work. When dreams are shattered and hope seems dead, work. Work as if your life were in peril. It really is. No matter what ails you, work. Work faithfully. . . . Work is the greatest remedy available for both mental and physical afflictions.[110]

Indeed, we would think that the first group of laborers would be grateful for the privilege to work. What a privilege to be an "all-day" laborer in the Lord's vineyard! What a privilege to have the light of the gospel constantly in our lives. Elder Packer made an interesting observation regarding seemingly mundane moments in our life which, when seen with the proper perspective, are actually rewarding reveries of spiritual nourishment:

> Before entering the temple to begin the ordinance work, the companies frequently will assemble in the chapel in the annex portion of the building. Here the members wait until the full company is assembled. *Generally in life we would become impatient with waiting. To be first in a room and then be compelled to wait for the last to enter before proceeding would in other circumstances cause irritation.* In the temple it is just the opposite. *That waiting is regarded as a choice opportunity.* What a privilege it is to sit quietly without conversation and direct the mind to reverent and spiritual thoughts! It is a refreshment to the soul.[111]

So it is with being a laborer in the vineyard for the whole day. It is not and should not be an "irritation" that we are "compelled" to go through. It can and should be regarded as a "choice opportunity."

---

110. Korsaren, *The Forbes Scrapbook of Thoughts on the Business of Life* (New York: Forbes, 1968) 427; quoted in J. Richard Clarke's "The Value of Work," *Ensign*, April 1982, 78.

111. Boyd K. Packer, *The Holy Temple* (Salt Lake City: Bookcraft, 1980), 58; emphasis added.

Furthermore, we would expect that the long-laboring workers would look with compassion on those who truly wanted to work but were genuinely unable. In this regard, it is worth noting that God can reward this last group equally with the first because of their willingness alone. We often misunderstand or completely ignore this aspect of the gospel. Dallin H. Oaks observed,

> When someone wanted to do something for my father-in-law but was prevented by circumstances, he would say, "Thank you. I will take the good will for the deed." Similarly, I believe that our Father in Heaven will receive the true desires of our hearts as a substitute for actions that are genuinely impossible. Here we see another contrast between the laws of God and the laws of men. It is entirely impractical to grant a legal advantage on the basis of an intent not translated into action. "I intended to sign that contract," or "We intended to get married," cannot stand as the equivalent of the act required by law. If the law were to give effect to intentions in lieu of specific acts, it would open the door for too much abuse, since the laws of man have no reliable means of determining our innermost thoughts. In contrast, the law of God can reward a righteous desire because an omniscient God can discern it. As revealed through the prophet of this dispensation, God "is a discerner of the thoughts and intents of the heart" (D&C 33:1). If a person refrains from a particular act because he is genuinely unable to perform it, but truly would if he could, our Heavenly Father will know this and will reward that person accordingly.[112]

This principle applies to those who seek to marry for eternity but cannot find a suitable partner. It applies to those who desire to serve in callings but are prevented by age or disabilities. And certainly, it applies to individuals who are seeking the truths of the restored gospel but "are only kept from the truth because they know not where to find it" (D&C 123:12). Here we begin to see the symbolism: "Because no man hath hired us." Or, "No one has taught us the gospel. We haven't found it yet, but we are so willing and ready!" Just because some laborers come into the Church later than lifelong members, we should not conclude that they deserve less of a reward.

---

112. Dallin H. Oaks, "The Desires of Our Hearts," *Ensign*, June 1986, 66.

Referring to the parable of the laborers in the vineyard, Dallin H. Oaks declared, "Like other parables, this one can teach several different and valuable principles." He then goes on to say,

> For present purposes its lesson is that the Master's reward in the Final Judgment will not be based on how long we have labored in the vineyard. We do not obtain our heavenly reward by punching a time clock. What is essential is that our labors in the workplace of the Lord have caused us to *become* something. For some of us, this requires a longer time than for others. What is important in the end is what we have become by our labors. Many who come in the eleventh hour have been refined and prepared by the Lord in ways other than formal employment in the vineyard. These workers are like the prepared dry mix to which it is only necessary to "add water"—the perfecting ordinance of baptism and the gift of the Holy Ghost. With that addition—even in the eleventh hour—these workers are in the same state of development and qualified to receive the same reward as those who have labored long in the vineyard. This parable teaches us that we should never give up hope and loving associations with family members and friends whose fine qualities evidence their progress toward what a loving Father would have them become. Similarly, the power of the Atonement and the principle of repentance show that we should never give up on loved ones who now seem to be making many wrong choices. Instead of being judgmental about others, we should be concerned about ourselves. We must not give up hope. We must not stop striving.[113]

We must not forget either that perhaps there are some laborers in Gods vineyard, in fact many, who labor for the kingdom without being formal members of the restored Church of Jesus Christ. Ezra Taft Benson said, "God, the Father of us all, uses the men of the earth, especially good men, to accomplish his purposes. It has been true in the past, it is true today, it will be true in the future."[114]

Similarly, Orson F. Whitney declared,

> Perhaps the Lord needs such men on the outside of His Church to help it along. They are among its auxiliaries, and can do more good for the cause where the Lord has placed them, than anywhere else. Hence, some are drawn into the fold and receive a testimony of the truth; while

113. Dallin H. Oaks, "The Challenge to Become," *Ensign*, Nov. 2000.
114. Ezra Taft Benson, "Civic Standards for the Faithful Saints," *Ensign*, July 1972, 59.

others remain unconverted, the beauties and glories of the gospel being veiled temporarily from their view, for a wise purpose. The Lord will open their eyes in His own due time. *God is using more than one people for the accomplishment of His great and marvelous work. The Latter-day Saints cannot do it all. It is too vast, too arduous for any one people.* We have no quarrel with the Gentiles. They are our partners in a certain sense.[115]

The Penny and Pride

Another interesting phrase is the following declaration: "When the first came, they supposed that they should have received more." The thought is ironic and even laughable in light of the symbolism: The penny, as said before, is eternal life—it is, in essence, to receive all that the Father Hath (D&C 84). It is to be a god, thus having all power and all knowledge. It is to have everything. What is the irony then? Simply this—we cannot receive more than eternal life, the greatest of all gifts. One cannot have any more than everything! "Here is your reward—everything!" says the Father. "But I want more!" exclaims the all-day laborer. The mind and heart are truly baffled at the thought. Again, we beg to question the true motives of this group that labored all day. It seems they were not so much concerned with receiving the reward and being content with it as they were to make sure they were ahead of—always and forever ahead of—those who labored for less hours. The focus is on status, not spiritual attainment.

C. S. Lewis accordingly observed,

> We say that people are proud of being rich, or clever, or good looking, but they are not. They are proud of being richer, or cleverer, or better-looking than others. If every one else became equally rich, or clever, or good-looking there would be nothing to be proud about. Pride gets no pleasure out of having something, only out of having more of it than the next man. . . . It is the comparison that makes you proud: the pleasure of being above the rest. Once the element of competition has gone, pride has gone.[116]

---

115. Orson F. Whitney, in Conference Report, Apr. 1928, 59; emphasis added.

116. Lewis, *Mere Christianity*, 102–10.

The spirit of entitlement has no place in God's Kingdom—here on earth or in Heaven.

Conclusion

The parable of the laborers in the vineyard is a timeless story with deep meaning for those with ears to hear and eyes to see. It is a powerful warning against the spirit of pride and entitlement. Additionally, it can help us see more clearly the doctrine of equality as it relates to God's eternal plan of salvation. Gender differences, gender roles, priesthood offices and keys, opportunities for leadership in the Church—all these need to be seen correctly through the lens of God's divine plan and eternal principles. Perhaps most important, the parable of the laborers in the vineyard is a potent statement and sublime testimony regarding the grace, mercy, and awesome power of the atoning sacrifice of our Lord and Savior, Jesus Christ. Indeed, it could just well be that the preferred way the Savior chose to teach about the multitudinous principles relating to His infinite Atonement was through the carefully cloaked statements contained in these seemingly simple stories of everyday life. The Lord told Enoch "all things have their likeness, and all things are created and made to bear record of me, both things which are temporal, and things which are spiritual" (Moses 6:63). So it is with the parable of the laborers in the vineyard.

Chapter 7

Marriage, Family, Balance, and Priorities

Friends, sweethearts, and spouses need to be able to monitor each other's stress and recognize the different tides and seasons of life. We owe it to each other to declare some limits and then help jettison some things if emotional health and the strength of loving relationships are at risk.[117]

—Jeffrey R. Holland

Many years ago, when my wife and I were in the first years of our marriage, I had a perplexing and poignant experience that caused me to deeply ponder and reflect on my priorities. I had just come home from work—tired and hungry, yet very excited. The reason for my excitement was that one of the local sports teams had a big game that would be televised that night. The game was starting just as I pulled into the driveway. I was in a hurry to get inside to watch it.

As I opened the door, I was greeted by my wife. Although I didn't realize it fully at the time, she was all dressed up and had done the same with our two-year-old daughter. Additionally, she had prepared a wonderful dinner with all the trimmings. The house had been cleaned spotlessly,

---

117. Jeffrey R. Holland, "How Do I Love Thee?," devotional, Brigham Young University, Feb. 15, 2000. See speeches.byu.edu.

and soft music was drifting through the air. To all of this thoughtful preparation I was completely oblivious. Little did I realize that she had prepared a wonderful evening just to express her love for me, as I would painfully realize a little later.

I quickly gave her a hug, asked in a somewhat casual way how her day had gone, and proceeded to go to the TV to turn on the game. I selected the station, and sure enough, the game had started. I loosened my tie, sat back on the sofa, and started taking in the game. Honestly, it took several minutes before I realized that she was still standing near the door where she greeted me, not watching the game, but watching me watch the game. I will never forget the disappointed look on her face. Although I would turn off the game and attempt a half-baked apology, the night (though not totally ruined) had been soured by my insensitive actions. The worst part of all was the discussion we had later that evening as she simply explained to me that she sometimes felt she was number two in my life. I was ashamed. My heart ached. I silently vowed that evening that some-how, someway, this would never happen again.

My experience that night caused me some serious soul searching. I knew my wife loved me, and I knew she knew I loved her. Yet, my actions have sometimes betrayed my expressions of love and commitment.

That night caused me to ask myself many questions. The questions were easy to ask, but their answers were much more difficult to obtain. They included such things as "What is our most important priority in life? Is it our Church calling? Is it our spouse, or children? Is it our occu-pation? Is it possible or even wise to rank these priorities?"

Frequently our choices in life consist of simple distinctions between good and evil. At other times, they do not. Often we find that deci-sion-making is actually fraught with perplexing choices between good vs. better, important vs. vital, and needful vs. essential. Perhaps this dilemma is one of the very reasons we come to this mortal sphere, despite the anxiety, to experience the interplay between time, talents, and agency. Fortunately, Latter-day prophets and Seers have given us ample guidance with these matters and have even taught in clear terms not only what our specific priorities should be but also how we can establish and balance them.

After the conclusion of an LDS Church Educational System (CES) fireside on February 5, 1999, Elder Jeffrey R. Holland of the Quorum of the Twelve Apostles gave additional counsel to CES faculty and guests that remained in the Assembly Hall on Temple Square. Among other things, he gave the following ranking of priorities that we should seek to establish in our lives:

1. Our own physical and spiritual needs
2. Our spouse's needs
3. Our children's needs
4. Our Church callings
5. Our professional life
6. Our civic responsibilities

Elder Holland assured those assembled that this list is nothing new and that prior prophets have taught the same. In 1972, President Harold B. Lee counseled, "Most men do not set priorities to guide them in allocating their time, and most men forget that *the first priority should be to maintain their own physical and spiritual strength.* Then comes their family, then the Church, and then their professions—and all need time."[118]

Our Spiritual Selves

It might seem perplexing to some to hear that our first priority is "ourselves." How can this be, especially when we have been counseled about the importance of family, not to mention the scriptural admonition that invites us to actually "lose ourselves" for others?

In 1994, President Howard W. Hunter gave this counsel: "*Your first obligation is to get your own spiritual life in order* through regular scripture study and daily prayer . . . [you should also] secure and honor your priesthood and temple covenants."[119]

Similarly, President Ezra Taft Benson has counseled, "To be successful, we must have the Spirit of the Lord. We have been taught that the Spirit will not dwell in unclean tabernacles. Therefore, *one of our first priorities is to make sure our own personal lives are in order.*"[120]

---

118. Harold B. Lee, *Bishop's Training Course and Self-Help Guide*, sec. 2, p. 7, as quoted in James E. Faust's "Happiness Is Having a Father Who Cares," *Ensign*, Jan. 1974, 23; emphasis added.
119. Howard W. Hunter, in Conference Report, Oct. 1994, 69; emphasis added.
120. Ezra Taft Benson, *Come unto Christ* (Salt Lake City: Deseret Book, 1983), 92.

As President Benson's and President Hunter's teachings infer, putting ourselves first is in reality the placing of God first, or, at least our relationship to him "through regular scripture study and daily prayer," etc. It is invoking our agency, through obedience, inviting the companionship, guidance, and cleansing effects of the Holy Ghost, thus assuring that the power of the Atonement of Jesus Christ is operative in our lives.

We often say that family is our number one priority, which is true, in a manner of speaking. "Family first!" is more than a motto. It is a doctrinal declaration of one of our most sublime values. Yet, as Elder Holland and President Lee suggest, one other thing is more important—our relationship with and obedience to God. President Russell M. Nelson puts into perspective the relationship between this first priority and the next two, our spouse and children, as follows:

> As we go through life, even through very rough waters, a father's instinctive impulse to cling tightly to his wife or to his children may not be the best way to accomplish his objective. Instead, if he will lovingly cling to the Savior and the iron rod of the gospel, his family will want to cling to him and to the Savior.[121]

This principle, properly applied, not only allows our loved ones to cling to and love us, but it also allows us to more fully love them. "Only when we love God above all others," taught Elder Marlin K. Jensen, "will we be capable of offering pure, Christlike love to our companions for all eternity."[122]

This placement of priorities should not be seen as a self-centered approach to living. Indeed, it is not. On the other hand, the Savior's admonition that we lose ourselves for others must be properly understood: "If any *man* will come after me, let him deny himself, and take up his cross, and follow me. For whosoever will save his life shall lose it: and whosoever will lose his life for my sake shall find it" (Matthew 16:24–25). The Joseph Smith translation of Matthew 16:26 gives us this clarifying detail: "And now for a man to take up his cross, is to deny himself all ungodliness, and every worldly lust and keep my commandments."

---

121. Russell M. Nelson, in Conference Report, Oct. 2001, 84.
122. Marlin K. Jensen, "A Union of Love and Understanding," *Ensign*, Oct. 1994, 46–51.

To deny ourselves does not mean we do not take appropriate care of our spiritual and physical selves. The appropriate placing of these things first is, as was said before, putting God first. Losing ourselves is, in reality, relinquishing *selfishness* and becoming what God would have us be. Elder Neal A. Maxwell gives these clarifying insights:

> Losing oneself means losing concern over getting credit; by knowing our true identity we need not be concerned about seeming anonymity. . . . Losing oneself means yielding the substance of one's own agendum if it does not match the agendum of the Lord. . . . Losing oneself means keeping ourselves more spiritually intact . . . so that we are able to help more. . . . Losing ourselves means being willing to go to Nineveh when we would much prefer to go to Tarshish . . . Losing oneself means losing one's impulsiveness. . . . Losing ourselves means dropping our resistance to feedback so that we can grow faster, just as did meek and receptive Moses, the brother of Jared, Peter, and Joseph Smith.[123]

Furthermore, we are not to lose ourselves in the sense that we give no care *at all* to our physical needs. Proponents of this thinking for example, especially those who would discredit and diminish physical exercise, might zealously quote 1 Timothy 4:8 wherein Paul counsels, "For bodily exercise profiteth *little*: but godliness is profitable unto all things" (emphasis added). Lest we misunderstand this scripture, the footnote in the LDS edition of the scriptures points out the Greek translation that renders the phrase this way: "Bodily exercise profiteth *a little while*" (emphasis added). This clarification bears out the principle that physical exercise is worthwhile, yet someday we will all be hindered by the aging process. If we can exercise, we should.

The Physical and Spiritual Self: A Divine Intermingling

To say that our spiritual self is our first priority is perhaps understandable, especially when considering it as a function of placing God and his commandments first. Yet to some it might appear odd to elevate one's physical well being to the same level. Nevertheless, latter-day revelation declares unequivocally the importance "of things both temporal and spiritual (1 Nephi 15:32)" in regard to the mortal soul. "The spirit *and* the

---

123. Neal A. Maxwell, *A Wonderful Flood of Light* (Salt Lake City, Utah: Bookcraft, 1990), 99.

body are the soul of man" and "spirit *and* element, *inseparably* connected, receive a fulness of joy; and when separated, man cannot receive a fulness of joy" (D&C 88:15; 93:33–34; see also D&C 45:17; 138:50). Both body and spirit blend together. One who is strong spiritually understands the importance of keeping his or her body as strong and as healthy as possible in order to serve God and man. It is difficult to give to others and serve them when we lack the health and vigor to do so. We are commanded not only to serve God with all our heart and mind, but we should also serve Him with all our might and strength (D&C 4:2; Moroni 10:32).

Physical discipline is a sign of being mentally clean. One who would control and expand his spiritual self knows the importance of controlling the physical self as well. Latter-day prophets and leaders have attested to this doctrine. President Spencer W. Kimball declared, "The highest achievement of spirituality comes as we conquer the flesh."[124]

President Harold B. Lee similarly taught, "Except [a man] learns to sacrifice his appetites and desires in obedience to the laws of the gospel [he] cannot be sanctified and made holy before the Lord."[125]

Spiritual attainment is thus a function, in part, of physical mastery. Elder Hartman Rector Jr. offered this insight as to the relationship that exists between body and spirit:

> It is primarily the spirit that sees, hears, feels, knows passion and desire; it is the spirit that becomes addicted to drugs, bad habits, and evil desires. It is not just the physical body that is addicted, but the spirit also, which, of course, is the real you and me. We are spirits just as God is a spirit. Sometimes we make excuses for ourselves, when we do what we should not do or fall short of what we should have done. We use such expressions as, "Oh! the spirit is willing but the flesh is weak." With such rationalizations we insinuate that it is completely our physical body's fault that we sin. In my opinion, this is not true. I believe the physical body is a very strong part of us and is of great benefit to us. Among other reasons, it was given to us to help us overcome our addictions, bad habits, and evil desires. The body is very obedient; generally speaking, it will do exactly what the spirit tells it to

---

124. Spencer W. Kimball, "And the Lord Called His People Zion," *Ensign*, Aug. 1984, 4.

125. Harold B. Lee, "For Every Child, His Spiritual and Cultural Heritage," *Children's Friend*, Aug. 1943, 373.

do. So it is not the physical body that we are struggling with; it is the spirit we must bring into subjection.[126]

The Dualistic Dimension of Discipleship

Obviously, we must be careful not to become too consumed with ourselves as we stress this first priority. We can focus so much on ourselves that we forget that there are other important priorities. Personal conversion is an end in itself, but it is also a means to an end. In fact, ultimate conversion and sanctification will not occur unless we realize the sobering fact that fully coming to Christ is dependent on helping others come to Him as well. This dualistic dimension of discipleship was eloquently taught by Joseph Smith in his epistle relative to the work for the deceased wherein he declared, "Their salvation is necessary and essential to our salvation . . . they without us cannot be made perfect—neither can we without our dead be made perfect" (D&C 128:15). The celestial kingdom will not be a place of spiritual seclusion where one finally escapes the mortal burden of caring for others.

"Service is not something we endure on this earth so we can earn the right to live in the celestial kingdom," said President Marion G. Romney. "Service is the very fiber of which an exalted life in the celestial kingdom is made."[127]

In essence, the two-fold design of the gospel is to come unto Christ ourselves and help others come unto Him. This includes helping Church members, nonmembers, and those who have died without having the opportunity to receive the fulness of the gospel. To Peter, the Lord tenderly but firmly taught the principle thus: "I have prayed for thee that thy faith fail not: and *when thou art converted, strengthen thy brethren*" (Luke 22:32). This dualistic dimension of our discipleship cannot be otherwise. The Psalmist declared,

> *Create in me a clean heart, O God; and renew a right spirit within me.* Cast me not away from thy presence; and take not thy holy spirit from me. Restore unto me the joy of thy salvation; and uphold me with thy free spirit. *Then will I teach* transgressors thy ways; and sinners shall be converted unto thee (Psalm 51:10–13, emphasis added; compare to D&C 11:21 and Joshua 1:11–15).

126. Hartman Rector Jr., in Conference Report, Oct. 1970, 73.
127. Romney, "The Celestial Nature of Self-Reliance," 93.

We have been commanded to share the gospel and to be a leaven to the world. We are to serve others and teach them the verities of eternity. To teach spiritual things effectively we must first be spiritually effective ourselves. "Very little love can come from one who is not at peace with himself or herself and God," said Elder Marlin K. Jensen. "No one can be concerned about the welfare of someone else and give love to another until he or she has taken care of his or her own soul."[128] Once we are converted, once we are grounded spiritually, we can and should help others do the same.

A Word of Caution

We must be careful, though, not to adopt the false notion that our spiritual lives can deteriorate while we still maintain the ability to help others spiritually; that we can help others gain and develop testimonies of the truth while not having done so ourselves. President Marion G. Romney taught that "spiritual guidance cannot come from the spiritually weak."[129]

Paul warned, "Thou therefore which teachest another, teachest thou not thyself?" (Romans 2:21). To assume that we can seek the salvation of others while disregarding our own, and that we will somehow receive an eternal reward for doing so, is to err.

The Book of Mormon chronicles the sad account of the seemingly helpful and promising Jaredite King named Morianton, who nobly helped others but did not help himself: "And after that he had established himself king he did ease the burden of the people, by which he did gain favor in the eyes of the people, and they did anoint him to be their king. And *he did do justice unto the people, but not unto himself* because of his many whoredoms; wherefore *he was cut off from the presence of the Lord*" (Ether 10:10–11, emphasis added; compare to Omni 1:1–2).

The converse is also true. Focusing on the salvation of others while disregarding our own won't do us much good, and neither will focusing on *our* salvation while disregarding that of others be of any benefit. In fact, the two are so intricately interwoven that it is difficult to separate them. Devotion to God, family, and others are not mutually exclusive categories. They are reinforcing and complementary. Elder John A. Widtsoe

---

128. Jensen, "A Union of Love and Understanding," 46–51.
129. Romney, "The Celestial Nature of Self-Reliance," 93.

declared this reality: "The Church is composed of homes. Church and home cannot be separated. Neither one comes first. They are one."[130]

Proper Balance

Elder M. Russell Ballard has counseled, "If you . . . search your hearts and courageously assess the priorities in your life, you may discover, as I did, that you need a better balance among your priorities."[131]

We must be careful not to make a mechanical and sequentially rigid list of personal priorities. To do so could be hazardous. "As always there must be balance," said Elder Neal A. Maxwell. "The inordinate reading of the living scriptures that crowded out one's family, one's neighbors, and Christian service would be an error. One could become monastic though scholastic. Christian service to mankind could crowd out the living scriptures and become so consuming that one could forget his duties to family and to God, being a do-gooder almost as an escape from the family framework."[132]

It is true that our spouse and children, although extremely important, are not our absolute highest priority, but this fact does not give us license to neglect (or abuse) them. Likewise, to nonchalantly say, "Well, my Church callings are priority number four, so I guess I can skip home teaching this month" is not in the spirit of what the prophets have taught either, since our priorities all need time. Certain things do need to be done at certain times in our lives. Additionally, we cannot simply force into our lives everything and anything that will possibly fit. Elder Holland captured this principle beautifully with the following analogy:

> As a youth in England, Samuel Plimsoll was fascinated with watching ships load and unload their cargoes. He soon observed that, regardless of the cargo space available, each ship had its maximum capacity. If a ship exceeded its limit, it would likely sink at sea. In 1868, Plimsoll entered Parliament and passed a merchant shipping act that, among other things, called for making calculations of how much a ship could carry. As a result, lines were drawn on the hull of each ship in England.

---

130. John A. Widtsoe, *Evidences and Reconciliations* (Salt Lake City: Bookcraft, 1943), 318.
131. M. Russell Ballard, "Keeping Life's Demands in Balance," *Ensign*, May 1987, 13.
132. Neal A. Maxwell, *Things As They Really Are* (Salt Lake City: Deseret Book, 1989), 106.

As the cargo was loaded, the freighter would sink lower and lower into the water. When the water level on the side of the ship reached the Plimsoll mark, the ship was considered loaded to capacity, regardless of how much space remained. As a result, British deaths at sea were greatly reduced.

Like ships, people have differing capacities at different times and even different days in their lives. In our relationships we need to establish our own Plimsoll marks and help identify them in the lives of those we love. Together we need to monitor the load levels and be helpful in shedding or at least readjusting some cargo if we see our sweetheart is sinking. Then, when the ship of love is stabilized, we can evaluate long-term what has to continue, what can be put off until another time, and what can be put off permanently. Friends, sweethearts, and spouses need to be able to monitor each other's stress and recognize the different tides and seasons of life. We owe it to each other to declare some limits and then help jettison some things if emotional health and the strength of loving relationships are at risk.[133]

Finding proper balance with our most important priorities is indeed challenging, especially when there are so many positive and worthwhile things we can do. Even the vigorous pursuit of what we would consider worthwhile objectives can be fraught with danger.

"Perpetual devotion to what a man calls his business is only to be sustained by perpetual neglect of many other things," said Robert Louis Stevenson, "and it is not by any means certain that a man's business is the most important thing he has to do."[134] Just because we are doing good things, we should not automatically assume we have our priorities straight. "Ironically, inordinate attention, even to good things, can diminish our devotion to God," counseled Elder Neal A. Maxwell. He taught,

> For instance, one can be too caught up in sports and the forms of body worship we see among us. One can reverence nature and yet neglect nature's God. One can have an exclusionary regard for good music and similarly with a worthy profession. In such circumstances, the "weightier matters" are often omitted (Matt. 23:23; see also 1 Cor. 2:16). Only the Highest One can fully guide us as to the highest good which you and I can do.[135]

133. Holland, "How Do I Love Thee?," 158–62.
134. Robert Louis Stevenson, *An Apology for Idlers* (New York City: Penguin, 2010).
135. Neal A. Maxwell, "Consecrate Thy Performance," *Ensign*, May 2002, 37.

Similarly, Elder Richard G. Scott warned,

Are there so many fascinating, exciting things to do or so many challenges pressing down upon you that it is hard to keep focused on that which is essential? When things of the world crowd in, all too often the wrong things take highest priority. Then it is easy to forget the fundamental purpose of life. Satan has a powerful tool to use against good people. It is distraction. He would have good people fill life with "good things" so there is no room for the essential ones. Have you unconscientiously been caught in that trap?[136]

We might have times in our lives when we innocently or naively mistake less important issues and activities as actually being vital values. C. S. Lewis portrayed the dilemma thus:

There have been men before now who got so interested in proving the existence of God that they came to care nothing for God Himself . . . as if the good Lord had nothing to do but *exist!* There have been some who were so occupied in spreading Christianity that they never gave a thought to Christ. Man! Ye see it in small matters. Did ye never know a lover of books that with all his first editions and signed copies had lost the power to read them? Or an organiser of charities that had lost all love for the poor? It is the subtlest of all the snares.[137]

We can get so consumed with how we present the gospel that the content, the message itself, is blurred. Appearance and aesthetics, no matter how wonderful and appealing, must never be substituted for nor be mistaken with substance and significance.

Conclusion

As stated before, the placing of our spiritual and physical selves first is in reality placing God first. President Ezra Taft Benson wisely counseled that "when we put God first, all other things fall into their proper place or drop out of our lives."[138] He also stated that "our love of the Lord will govern the claims for our affection, the demands on our time, the interests

---

136. Richard G. Scott, "First Things First," *Ensign*, May 2001, 6.
137. C. S. Lewis, *The Great Divorce* (New York: Harper Collins 2001), 73–74.
138. Ezra Taft Benson, "The Great Commandment," *Ensign*, May 1988, 4.

we pursue, and the order of our priorities."[139] What a promise! If we are struggling to prioritize, we just need to put our first priority first. All other priorities will fall into place as they should. It is really that simple.

Yet, at times, we can unconsciously or even knowingly insist on making our pursuit of spirituality a complex and arduous undertaking. To some the thought of putting God first can appear burdensome. Occasionally we hear this statement, supposedly made by the Savior and even regarded as scripture to some: "I never said it would be easy, I only said it would be worth it."

Perhaps many comprehend the essence of this statement and even go so far as to mount it on their wall. However, two things are of note. First, the Savior, at least in scripture, never did say this. Second, as nice and motivational as it might sound, this statement is not necessarily true. In fact, the opposite proves to be true in the words of the Master: "Take my yoke upon you . . . My yoke *is easy*, and my burden is light" (Matthew 11:29–30; emphasis added).

Alma reminded his son Helaman that it is "easy to give heed to the word of Christ, which will point to you a straight course to eternal bliss" (Alma 37:46). Similarly, John extols that God's "commandments are not grievous" (1 John 5:3).

This does not mitigate the fact that there are many people striving with all their hearts to live the gospel, who still might have deep pains and heavy burdens from life. Yet it is nonetheless true that putting God first in our lives is actually easier than anything we would do otherwise. Elder A. Theodore Tuttle reminded us of this principle when he explained that God's commandments "are for our good, and when we violate them, we suffer spiritually, physically, and emotionally. Remember . . . it's not nearly as hard to live the commandments as not to live them. The burden of keeping the commandments of the Lord is light compared to the burden of sin which we carry when we violate the commandments of God."[140]

May we all strive to do the will of the Lord, to feed ourselves spiritually, thus activating the power of the Atonement in our lives, and then, to the best of our ability, help our spouses, children, friends, and neighbors do likewise.

"The most important principle I can share," Elder Richard G. Scott declared, is to "anchor your life in Jesus Christ, your Redeemer. Make

---

139. Ibid.
140. Theodore A. Tuttle, in Conference Report, Oct. 1965, 32.

your Eternal Father and his Beloved Son the most important priority in your life—more important than life itself, more important than a beloved companion or children or anyone on earth. Make their will your central desire. Then all that you need for happiness will come to you."[141]

141. Richard G. Scott, "The Power of Correct Principles," *Ensign*, May 1993, 34.

To those whom God should call in the last days, who should hold the power of priesthood to bring again Zion, and the redemption of Israel; and to put on her strength is to put on the authority of the priesthood, which she, Zion, has a right to by lineage; also to return to that power which she had lost.

—DC 113:8

Part 3

WOMEN, THE TEMPLE, AND ETERNITY

Chapter 8

Our Destiny: Becoming Kings and Queens

Remember that that which cometh from above is sacred, and must be spoken with care, and by constraint of the Spirit; and in this there is no condemnation.

—Doctrine and Covenants 63:64

Why speakest thou unto them in parables? He answered and said unto them, because it is given unto you to know the mysteries of the kingdom of heaven, but to them it is not given. . . . Therefore speak I to them in parables: because they seeing see not; and hearing they hear not, neither do they under-stand. . . . But blessed are your eyes, for they see: and your ears, for they hear.

—Matthew 13:10–16

The temple is a place of holiness. It is a place of introspective instruc-tion and light-filled learning. It is a timeless tutorial that uses sacred symbols often and overtly to point God's children to their potential and perpetual destiny. These symbols not only reveal God's doctrine, but they conceal it as well.

John the Revelator spoke somewhat cryptically of our eternal potential as follows: "To him that overcometh will I grant to sit with me in *my
throne*, even as I also overcame, and am set down with my *Father in his
throne*. He that hath an ear, let him hear what the Spirit saith" (Revelation
3:21–22, emphasis added).

The notion of obtaining a throne, of being crowned, of becoming
kings and queens is central to the theology and symbolism of God's holy
house. In fact, these regnal references not only denote salvation but are
also directly symbolic of eternal life, which is exaltation in the highest
degree of heaven in the celestial glory.

Elder Bruce R. McConkie commented on the symbolism of being
crowned: "Those who gain exaltation in the highest heaven of the celestial
world *shall wear crowns*. Perhaps literal crowns may be worn on occasion—emblematic of their victory over the world and signifying that *they
rule and reign as kings and queens in the eternal house of Israel.*"[142]

Whether those crowns are literal remains to be seen in some future
day. Regardless, the Lord has revealed the figurative nature of these
crowns: "If ye are faithful ye shall be laden with many sheaves, and
crowned with honor, and glory, and immortality, and eternal life" (Doctrine
and Covenants 75:5, emphasis added). This noble ideal is not only central
to the temple, but to the very essence of Heavenly Father's eternal plan
as well.

President Spencer W. Kimball reminded us that "We do not rear children just to please our vanity. We bring children into the world *to become
kings and queens, priests and priestesses for our Lord.*"[143]

Lorenzo Snow pleaded with the Saints to "conduct yourselves with
prudence in all things, and labor for the interests of the kingdom of God,
and that we may not be among the foolish virgins, but be found worthy
to be amongst those who will be crowned as *kings and queens and reign
throughout eternity.*"[144]

Such individuals receive eternal increase. They receive "all power"
and the "continuation of the seeds" (D&C 132:19–20). They receive the

---

142. McConkie, *Mormon Doctrine*, 173. See also *The Doctrine and Covenants Student
Manual*, Religion 324 and 325, "Neither Be Idle but Labor with Your Might,"
156.

143. Spencer W. Kimball, *The Doctrine and Covenants Student Manual*, Religion 324
and 325, "Truth Is Knowledge of Things . . . ," 217.

144. *Teachings of Presidents of the Church: Lorenzo Snow* [2012], "Reflections on the
Mission of Jesus Christ," 277; emphasis added.

"father's kingdom" and "all that the Father hath" (D&C 84:33–38). They are filled "with His glory" and are "made equal with Him" (D&C 88:107). They become "joint heirs" with Christ (Romans 8:17) and they "sit in His throne" (Revelation 3:21). In short, they become gods and goddesses and kings and queens. This is the meaning and scope of all regnal references in the scriptures.

The idea of becoming a king or queen, in a symbolic, spiritual, or eternal sense is intriguing. The notion that the faithful "shall inherit thrones, kingdoms, principalities, and powers, dominions, all heights and depths" (D&C 132:19) is entrancing and enthralling. There is an allure of sorts that we feel—an attraction to this lofty aspiration. It seems that many people in the world today (and throughout history) have a fascination with royalty and regalia, with kingdoms and crowns and princes and princesses. Whether it's through the tabloid news or fairytales of old, the concept of hereditary nobility captures the imagination and inspires a longing to "live happily ever after." It is thus intriguing to consider that the Lord has commanded his children to not only obtain instruction "in principle, in doctrine, in the law of the gospel, [and] in all things that pertain unto the kingdom of God," but also instruction regarding "the wars and the perplexities of the nations, and the judgments which are on the land; and *a knowledge also of countries and of kingdoms*" (D&C 88:78–79; emphasis added). Likewise, the Lord has declared, "Verily I say unto you, that it is my will that you should hasten to translate my scriptures, and *to obtain a knowledge of history, and of countries, and of kingdoms*, of laws of God and man, *and all this for the salvation of Zion*" (Doctrine and Covenants 93:53).

Why would the Lord want us to have knowledge of earthly kingdoms? That is an intriguing question indeed. It should be noted that Mormonism doesn't claim to be a "new" religion but a "restored" religion—a religion that was anciently here on earth in its fulness from the foundation of the world (see D&C 128:18). Because of multiple periods of apostasy, such a reality would naturally leave a trail of theological debris in other altered (or otherwise corrupted) religious and philosophical systems throughout the history of mankind. Perhaps the Lord wants us to study these earthly kingdoms and systems not only to avoid the mistakes of history, but also to enlighten and instruct us. Perhaps He wants us to unlock the symbols of our own sacred theology through the preserved, albeit tainted, allegories of antiquity. Although we cannot discuss specific details of certain aspects of the temple endowment ceremony due to their sacred nature, we can draw parallels between the endowment and the coronation ceremony of monarchs.

Coronation of Kings and Queens

Various countries and peoples have established and enacted coronation ceremonies over the centuries and millennia past in order to distinguish and proclaim the reign of earthly kings and queens. Many of these ceremonies claim precedence from the holy scriptures. The form of coronation between cultures and countries is similar, as should be expected, since many of these ceremonies once had a common source. However there are some differences. The following is a basic summary of the most common elements of the coronation of kings and queens. As the reader gains "a knowledge also of countries and of kingdoms" herein, it is hoped that ears will indeed hear and eyes will be opened. Furthermore, it is hoped that the reader will be able to relate to this statement made by Joseph Smith as it applies to the holy temples and their associated system of gospel instruction: "Our minds being now enlightened, we began to have the scriptures laid open to our understandings, and the true meaning and intention of their more mysterious passages revealed unto us in a manner which we never could attain to previously, nor ever before had thought of" (Joseph Smith—History 1:74).

Procession of Guests into Sacred Rooms or Edifices

Coronation and other enthronement rites often begin with processions (or marches) which can included the entrance of royalty, heads of state, and other invited guests into the chapels, halls, cathedrals, or sacred rooms that are prepared for the coronation ceremonies. Sacred music often accompanies this initial stage of the service, including the singing of anthems, which are often based on scriptural or liturgical texts. An example from the British coronation is the singing of the anthem from Psalm 122:1, which includes the phrase, "I was glad when they said unto me: We will go into the house of the Lord." Such anthems and music help contribute to the ambiance and aesthetic atmosphere that is desired to prepare the invited guests for the occasion at hand.

Coronation of Emperor Nicholas II of Russia and Empress Alexandra
Feodorovna in 1896. The king and queen at the altar, the men
of the court to the right, and the women to the left in veils.
Painting by Laurits Tuxen (1853–1927).

Receiving a New Name

Kings and queens, popes and princes, and sovereigns and monarchs commonly receive a new name when they ascend to the throne or are elected to office. Often this new name is referred to as the regnal or reign name. For popes it is referred to as the papal name. In ancient Egypt, pharaohs received a "throne name" as opposed to the "temple name" as it is often referred to in East Asia and the orient. This new name is scripturally, genealogically, hereditarily, or historically based and is given and used to remind the monarch and those he serves of his or her change in title, status, and function as an empowered servant to benefit his or her subordinates. The practice of giving a new name dates back to ancient times and has occurred even with laity or non-royal members of religious congregations, often referred to as ones "religious name" or "spiritual name."

Washings and Anointings

Washings and/or anointings are often performed in the beginning of the coronation ceremony. This part of the coronation or enthronement rite claims ancient roots dating back to biblical times. An example of this from the Bible is found in Exodus:

> And Aaron and his sons thou shalt bring unto the door of the tabernacle of the congregation, and *shalt wash them with water*. And thou shalt take the garments, and put upon Aaron the coat, and the robe of the ephod, and the ephod, and the breastplate, and gird him with the curious girdle of the ephod: And thou shalt put the mitre upon his head, and put the holy crown upon the mitre. Then shalt thou *take the anointing oil, and pour it upon his head, and anoint him*. And thou shalt bring his sons, and put coats upon them. And thou shalt gird them with girdles, Aaron and his sons, and put the bonnets on them. (Exodus 29:4–9; emphasis added)

When Queen Elizabeth II ascended to the British throne in 1952, a prayer was uttered by the Archbishop which included these words:

> O Lord and heavenly Father, the exalter of the humble and the strength of thy chosen, who by anointing with Oil didst of old make and consecrate kings, priests, and prophets, to teach and govern thy people Israel: Bless and sanctify thy chosen servant . . . , who by our office and ministry is now to be anointed with this Oil . . . Strengthen her, O Lord, with the Holy Ghost the Comforter; Confirm and stablish her with thy free and princely Spirit.

At this point in the ceremony, Elizabeth sat down in King Edward's Chair to be anointed. The Dean of Westminster poured some holy oil into the filigreed spoon, and with it the Archbishop anointed the Queen's head, palms, and breast with holy oil. The palms of both hands are blessed with the words, "Be thy Hands anointed with holy Oil." The breast is blessed by saying, "Be thy Breast anointed with holy Oil." And finally, the crown of the head includes these words of dedication, "Be thy Head anointed with holy Oil: as kings, priests, and prophets were anointed: . . . you may at last be made partaker of an eternal kingdom, through the same Jesus Christ our Lord. Amen."

Whereas the British coronation ceremony involves anointing three places (head, palms, and breast), the French coronation has five places of anointing. In this case, the French monarch removes all clothing, except for a long shirt and stands barefoot to receive the anointing on the hands, within the breast, between the shoulders, in the break of the arm (the elbow), and on the head in the manner of a cross with the holy oil.

Alonzo Gaskill surmises that "the washing with water cleansed the initiate and prepared him or her to receive the Holy Spirit, which was typically symbolized among the ancients by the act of anointing with oil from a horn." The acts of washing and then anointing can be seen as symbols of Christ, "whose title literally means 'anointed one.' Hence, to be washed lead to an anointing, and to be anointed suggested that one was God's representative. The rite was, in the very least, a commitment on the part of the initiate to live and minister as God would."[145]

To be covered so completely in oil serves as a reminder that it is "only in and through the grace of God that [we] are saved" (2 Nephi 10:24). Royalty, in the ancient worldly setting, was something that was usually inherited and not earned or purchased. Thus it is that becoming a king or a queen, in a spiritual or eternal sense, is an honor that is not merited or earned. It is a right bestowed through the mercy and grace of Christ to those who are accepting of He whose crown it is to give to those willing to receive. Enoch readily understood this truth. He said, "Thou hast made me, *and given unto me a right to thy throne*, and not of myself, *but through thine own grace*" (Moses 7:59).

Preliminary Clothing in Plain White Garments

After the washing and anointing portion of the enthronement or coronation ceremony, the monarch receives and is clothed in a simple, plain white linen undergarment called the Colobium Sindonis. This unadorned garment symbolizes divesting oneself of vanity, eschewing all things worldly, and standing bare before God. During the Coronation of Elizabeth II, the Queen sat down in King Edward's Chair, whereupon the Dean of Westminster, assisted by a female attendant, put upon the British Monarch the Colobium Sindonis (Latin for "shroud tunic"). Further clothing is received, all preliminary to the final clothing in royal robes.

---

145. Alonzo Gaskill, *Sacred Symbols* (Springville, UT: Cedar Fort, 2011), 40.

*Queen Elizabeth II being clothed in the plain white
undergarment known as the Colobium Sindonis (1952)*

Papal Coronation and kneeling before the altar

Kneeling before the Altar and
Taking of Oaths and Promises

At this point, the monarch is brought before the altar, where a bible (or other holy texts) and other various items of familial significance are placed. Solemn oaths are taken and entered into, often prefaced with the following phrase as the charge is given to the royal initiate: "Will you solemnly promise and swear to . . ." and "Will you, to the utmost of your power, maintain the laws of God and the true profession of the gospel?" The charges and oaths administered and entered into are numerous and sacred, often involving commitment to God's laws, service to one's fellow beings, and one's own self-comportment.

Clothing in Royal Robes

Royal robes are received by the monarch and, depending on the point in the ceremony, are often placed on certain shoulders, sometimes being switched later in the ceremony to the other shoulder. During the coronation of Elizabeth II, these words of instruction were given by the archbishop: "Receive this Imperial Robe, and the Lord God endue [endow] you with knowledge and wisdom, with majesty and power from on high; *the Lord clothe you with the robe of righteousness, and with the garments of salvation.* Amen" (emphasis added).[146] The symbolism here is straightforward and intriguing. The language here, parsed from Isaiah, indicates a robe of "righteousness," perhaps serving as a reminder to the royal initiate that righteousness is not a function of an internal production or effort but rather a reception of an external source.

Receiving and Holding Various Items of Regalia

During a coronation, various items of regalia are given to and received by the monarch. Typical items include, among other things, an orb, the sword of state, the royal ring (signet ring), the scepter, and a crown. The sword of state (also known as the sword of justice or mercy), is one of the first items received and is sometimes lifted and held forward in the right hand, with the right arm to the square. In other ceremonies, depending on the nation, the sword is held with two hands and represents the power

---

146. See Isaiah 61:10.

of a monarch to defend his or her country against their enemies. It also symbolizes ultimate jurisdictional power. The orb, usually surmounted with a cross, typifies Christ's reign over the earth, thus symbolizing the bestowal and reception of celestial reward (such as "the meek shall inherit the earth"—see Matthew 5:5). The monarch receives the orb by placing the hand underneath the orb in cupping shape. At the beginning of the coronation ceremony, the orb is delivered into the Monarch's right hand. The orb is then placed on the altar where it remains until the end of the ceremony. At the conclusion, the Monarch holds the orb in the left hand, while holding the scepter in the right hand. The ring is a symbol of the authority and power of the monarch and is received by placing the right hand forward with the palm turned down. The archbishop places the ring on the fourth finger of the monarch's right hand.

First-century statue of Jupiter in the Hermitage (left), with robe on the left shoulder, holding the scepter in the left hand with arm to the square, and the right hand in cupping shape underneath the orb. Other kings and emperors (such as the roman emperor to the right) receive various items of regalia in similar fashion.

Queen Elizabeth II (above) fully clothed at the end of coronation—
orb and scepter switched as is customary, with the ring on her right finger.

Crowning of the Monarch

The culminating act of the enthronement, or coronation ceremony, is the reception of the crown. In the British coronation, the archbishop holds the crown with both hands, high above the head of the monarch, and places the crown on the monarch, while the congregation exults in a united voice three times: "God save the King! God save the King! God save the King!" The congregation immediately follows the crowning of the monarch by placing coronets and caps on their heads. In some enthronement ceremonies, the monarch receives the crown with both hands outstretched, high above their head, lowering the crown three times on their head. Often in coronation and enthronement ceremonies, this scripture in Psalms is recited as follows: "Let my prayer come up into thy presence as the incense: and let *the lifting up of my hands be as an evening sacrifice.* Alleluia" (Psalms 141:2; emphasis added).

It is interesting to note that during a relatively short period of time during the Middle Ages, some European Kings elected to have their heirs apparent anointed and crowned during their own lifetime in order to avoid succession disputes. This practice was seen in England, France, and Hungary, to name a few. These heirs didn't become royalty in the moment of the coronation, yet they were anointed and crowned to become such one day, depending on their faithfulness in fulfilling the vows of office and living to fulfill their destined vocation. These junior kings had very little authority and could not exercise the full power of office until the day came when they actually ascended to the throne as the reigning monarchs of their nations.

Apocryphal depiction of the Archangel Raphael
("he who heals"), sometimes associated with or as being
a dispensation head—probably Enoch (see D&C 128:21).

This central figure is fully clothed with the robe on his right shoulder,
the scepter in his right hand with his arm to the square, and
the orb in his left hand, which is in cupping shape underneath.

111

To Thy Throne We'll Come

Come and wash us, oh Jehovah, Zion's King, with water pure.
Cleanse our stains; pronounce us holy. Ancient promises assure!
Cover us with oil unblemished, as thy blood did freely flow—
Head and arms and back to strengthen, eyes and ears thy truth to know.

Clothe us with the Spirit Holy; robes of righteousness bestow
Gird us now with life eternal, seeds forevermore to sow.
Royal sons and daughters make us who before thy throne do bow.
Swords of truth we'll raise before us, in remembrance of our vow.

Lord, dost Thou the earth now grant us—orbs celestial, promised lands?
Scepter of divine dominion wilt Thou place in outstretched hands?
Ring of power, ring eternal? Gifts of mercy, gifts of grace!
Grateful hands we reach to heaven; in truth's round we seek thy face.

Thou hast covered us completely; Thou the prize hast won alone.
Thou prepar'dst the way before for us to sit with Thee on thy throne.
Come, bestow thy crown, Jehovah! Thrice we raise our voice to Thee!
To thy throne we'll come most boldly throughout all eternity!

—C. Robert Line

Chapter 9

Women, the Temple, and Wearing the Veil

Every ordinance of the gospel focuses in one way or another on the Atonement of the Lord Jesus Christ.

—*Jeffrey R. Holland*

*I*n the temple during the endowment, female patrons wear a veil, which has profound Atonement symbolism. Unfortunately, some women do not see or understand this, and even may erroneously feel that they are being treated differently than the men and perhaps even demeaned by this article of clothing, feeling that some unjustified message of subservience is being sent. Nothing could be further from the truth. To understand at least one level of symbolism inherent in the wearing of the veil (and its connection to the Atonement), it may be helpful to understand some of the writings of Paul. In his epistle to the Ephesians, Paul speaks of the sacred relationship of husband and wife, comparing it to the relationship between Christ and the Church.

> Wives, submit yourselves unto your own husbands, as unto the Lord. *For the husband is the head of the wife, even as Christ is the head of the church*: and he is the saviour of the body. Therefore as the church is subject unto Christ, so let the wives be to their own husbands in

113

everything. Husbands, love your wives, even as Christ also loved the church, and gave himself for it. (Ephesians 5:22–25, emphasis added)

To understand the veil motif, we must understand that Paul is comparing the man to Christ and the woman to the Church. In the temple endowment, we could say that the women there present, in a limited way, represent not just women, but the whole Church—men included! With this in mind, let us now examine another statement from Paul. In his second epistle to the Corinthian Saints, Paul gives this interesting counsel with regard to the wearing of the veil:

> But if the ministration of death, written and engraven in stones, was glorious, so that the *children of Israel could not steadfastly behold the face of Moses for the glory of his countenance*; which glory was to be done away: How shall not the ministration of the spirit be rather glorious? For if the ministration of condemnation be glory, much more doth the ministration of righteousness exceed in glory. For even that which was made glorious had no glory in this respect, by reason of the glory that excelleth. For if that which is done away was glorious, much more that which remaineth is glorious. Seeing then that we have such hope, we use great plainness of speech: And not as *Moses, which put a veil over his face,* that the children of Israel could not steadfastly look to the end of that which is abolished: *But their minds were blinded: for until this day remaineth the same veil untaken away in the reading of the old testament; which veil is done away in Christ.* But even unto this day, when Moses is read, *the veil is upon their heart.* Nevertheless when it shall turn to the Lord, the veil shall be taken away. (2 Corinthians 3:7–16; emphasis added)

The idea here is similar to the symbolism we see regarding the veil of the temple itself, which represents the law of justice—a barrier which keeps us from seeing or beholding God.[147] It is as though the wearing of the veil symbolically reminds all of us (not just women) that we are all veiled from entering God's presence, unless Christ removes the veil. Only he can satisfy the demands of justice, thus allowing us to enter back into the Father's presence.

---

147. C. Robert Line, *Endowed with Power: How Temple Symbols Guide Us to Christ's Atonement* (Springville, UT: Cedar Fort, 2017), 64–65.

It is interesting that in a non-LDS wedding ceremony (if and when a wedding veil is used), the man, not the woman lifts the veil from the bride's face. So it is that Christ, the bridegroom, is the one who removes the veil (the law of justice) so that all of us, if we so choose, can gain access to Heavenly Father's presence again. One Christian scholar made this observation:

> Not only does the bridal veil show the modesty and purity of the bride and her reverence for God, but it also reminds us of the Temple veil which was torn in two when Christ died on the cross. The removing of the veil took away the separation between God and man, giving believers access into the very presence of God. Since Christian marriage is a picture of the union between Christ and the church, we see another reflection of this relationship in the removal of the bridal veil. Through marriage, the couple now has full access to one another.[148]

The Doctrine and Covenants is replete with veil symbolism. Notice how each reference below deals with the spiritual blindness that we, both men and women, face on earth, which can only be removed by Christ, the bridegroom.

"The veil of darkness shall soon be rent." (D&C 38:8)

"The veil shall be rent and you shall see me." (D&C 67:10)

"The veil of the covering of my temple . . . shall be taken off." (D&C 101:23)

"The veil was taken from our minds." (D&C 110:1)

In none of these instances, nor in the Bible, is there exclusive mention of the veil being an article of clothing that is designated for women only. No, it is a symbol that represents the impeding cover (law of justice) which needs to be and can be removed from all of us but only through Jesus Christ's infinite Atonement.

---

148. Mary Fairchild, "Christian Wedding Customs and Traditions," as found on the Learn Religion website. See christianity.about.com; accessed August 5, 2019.

Chapter 10

Heavenly Antecedents: Womanhood, Motherhood, and Priesthood as Preparations for Eternity

As we conclude this book, it might be helpful to discuss a related doctrine that applies to everything we do here in mortality, including and especially, motherhood, womanhood, and the priesthood. These are all preparations for the next life. In the same way that the Aaronic Priesthood is a preparatory priesthood (see D&C 107:1–10), it could likewise be said that the Melchizedek Priesthood is also preparatory for the next life. In fact, much of what we do here in mortality is preparatory, and only a microcosm for what lies ahead. How sad it is that some of us become hung up on the brief blip that is mortality, little realizing what greater and more grandeur things lie ahead. To better understand how womanhood, motherhood, and the priesthood are all preparations for the next life, we must first understand some principles relating to an important law taught in the Book of Mormon. It is called the law of restitution.

In Alma 41, the prophet Alma gives a concise and powerful definition of and an associated discourse on the law of restoration. It could be said that this law is preeminent in the gospel of Jesus Christ. For one thing, Alma equates this law with the plan of salvation itself, calling it "the plan of restoration" (Alma 41:2). This law, in its scriptural context, has little or nothing to do with the restoration of the gospel per se, and it is not confined solely to a nuanced expression of the doctrine of the resurrection, though it gets closer to the point. The aim of this article will be to more accurately define Alma's meaning of *restoration* and to show that a correct understanding of this law can help Heavenly Father's children better comprehend how the multitude of trials, follies, and experiences of this life prepare us for the next—even eternal life.

Alma's Law of Restoration in Context

The law of restoration, as taught by Alma to his son Corianton in Alma 41, finds its roots in the beginning of Alma's discourse to his wayward son in Alma 39.[149] There he teaches the following preliminary and related concepts, such as some choices, particularly evil ones, can have severe consequences, even lasting into the next life: "Ye cannot hide your crimes from God; and except ye repent they will stand as a testimony against you at the last day" (Alma 39:6–8). He also warns that some things will not be restored to us in the next life, like monetary riches (Alma 39:14).

At the end of chapter 40, Alma begins to describe the resurrection as the "restoration of those things of which has been spoken by the mouths of the prophets" (v. 22; emphasis added). This shift carries over into Alma 41, where Alma mentions "restoration" or "restored" seventeen times; however, he only mentions "resurrection" once:

"Yea, this bringeth about the restoration of those things of which has been spoken by the mouths of the prophets. The soul shall be restored to the body, and the body to the soul; yea, and every limb and joint shall be restored to its body; yea, even a hair of the head shall not be lost; but all things shall be restored to their proper and perfect frame" (Alma

---

149. It should be noted that Alma does use the word "restoration" in Alma 37:19 when counseling his son Helaman, though the usage here appears independent from and unrelated to the context of the term in Alma's counsel to his son Corianton in Alma 39–42.

40:22–23).[150] Although resurrection is part of the law of restoration, it is only a small part. There is more.

The real gist of Alma's instruction on this law is simple and direct: the things we do will come back to us, all things in fact.

"I say unto thee, my son, that the plan of restoration is requisite with the justice of God; for it is requisite that *all things should be restored to their proper order*" (Alma 41:2; emphasis added). At its heart, we see similarities to the Pauline "Law of the Harvest" theology: "Be not deceived; God is not mocked: for whatsoever a man soweth, that shall he also reap" (Galatians 6:7). In colloquial terms we would say, "Whatever goes around comes around."

Alma often and repeatedly reminds his son that *restoration* is not to be equated with unmerited *transformation:* "Do not suppose, because it has been spoken concerning restoration, that ye shall be restored from sin to happiness. Behold, I say unto you, wickedness never was happiness" (Alma 41:10). In summary, "That which ye do send out shall return unto you again, and be restored; therefore, the word restoration more fully condemneth the sinner, and justifieth him not at all" (Alma 41:15).

Additionally, Alma seems to take this law of restoration a step further than the Golden Rule. It is more than just, "Do unto others as you would have them do unto you," but, "What you do unto others will eventually be done unto you!" Alma's teaching to Corianton is clear on this point: "The meaning of the word restoration is to bring back again evil for evil, or carnal for carnal, or devilish for devilish—good for that which is good; righteous for that which is righteous; just for that which is just; merciful for that which is merciful" (Alma 41:13).

Also inherent in the law of restoration is a magnifying effect. This is to say that a righteous individual is more than just "restored" to good. He or she is likewise rewarded. In Alma we read, "If ye do all these things then shall *ye receive your reward*; yea, ye shall have mercy restored unto you again; ye shall have justice restored unto you again; ye shall have a righteous judgment restored unto you again; and *ye shall have good rewarded unto you again*" (Alma 41:14).

This is similar to what Alma teaches Corinaton's brother Helaman in a different though related topic when he reminds his son "that by small

---

150. Soul in this instance is probably best understood as the spirit (in context) as opposed to the more common definition of soul in D&C 88:15.

and simple things are great things brought to pass; and small means in many instances doth confound the wise" (Alma 37:6).

C. S. Lewis observed,

> Good and evil both increase at compound interest. That is why the little decisions you and I make every day are of such infinite importance. The smallest good act today is the capture of a strategic point from which, a few months later, you may be able to go on to victories you never dreamed of. An apparently trivial indulgence in lust or anger today is the loss of a ridge or railway line or bridgehead from which the enemy may launch an attack otherwise impossible.[151]

This magnifying effect in the law of restoration can also be seen in the Savior's famous teaching found in the parable of the talents in Matthew 25. It did not matter how many talents each servant was given initially, only that they were faithful in using for good that which they were given.

To those with few talents or many, the reward is the same as the other faithful servants and is greater than both the amount each was given initially. It is likewise greater than the amount they ended with: "Well done, thou good and faithful servant: thou hast *been faithful over a few things*, I will make thee ruler *over many things*: enter thou into the joy of thy lord" (Matthew 25:21, 23).

Desires and the Law of Restoration

It has been said, "The road to hell is paved with good intentions."[152] Although clever and captivating, this saying is doctrinally dubious. Alma's law of restoration, while clearly teaching the necessity and importance of our actions, also acknowledges that desires and the intentions matter in God's plan.

"And it is requisite with the justice of God that men should be judged according to their works; and if their works were good in this life, *and the desires of their hearts were good*, that they should also, at the last day, be restored unto that which is good" (Alma 41:3, emphasis added). These "desires of our heart" are efficacious and can likewise serve as evidence as to our righteousness, despite the lack of accompanying works.

---

151. Lewis, *Mere Christianity*.
152. Often attributed to Cistercian abbot Saint Bernard of Clairvaux (1090–1153). See phrases.org; accessed August 5, 2019.

Alma reminds us, "The one raised to happiness *according to his desires of happiness*, or good according to his *desires of good*; and the other to evil *according to his desires of evil*; for *as he has desired to do evil all the day long even so shall he have his reward* of evil when the night cometh" (Alma 41:5; emphasis added).

The law of restoration desires count. This is made clear, in at least one sense, in that we are taught that we will be held accountable for and punished for evil desires and thoughts. The scriptures teach, "But this much I can tell you, that if ye do not watch yourselves, and your thoughts, and your words, and your deeds, and observe the commandments of God, and continue in the faith of what ye have heard concerning the coming of our Lord, even unto the end of your lives, ye must perish. And now, O man, remember, and perish not" (Mosiah 4:30; see also Matthew 15:18).

Isn't it reasonable to conclude the opposite? This is to say, if God can (and does) punish evil desires and thoughts, would he not likewise reward righteous thoughts and desires?

As quoted earlier in this book, here is what Elder Dallin H. Oaks said about the righteous desires of our hearts. It is a comforting reminder that our Heavenly Father is aware of us and knows the intents of our hearts:

> When someone wanted to do something for my father-in-law but was prevented by circumstances, he would say, "Thank you. I will take the good will for the deed." Similarly, I believe that our Father in Heaven will receive the true desires of our hearts as a substitute for actions that are genuinely impossible. Here we see another contrast between the laws of God and the laws of men. It is entirely impractical to grant a legal advantage on the basis of an intent not translated into action. "I intended to sign that contract," or "We intended to get married," cannot stand as the equivalent of the act required by law. If the law were to give effect to intentions in lieu of specific acts, it would open the door for too much abuse, since the laws of man have no reliable means of determining our innermost thoughts. In contrast, *the law of God can reward a righteous desire because an omniscient God can discern it*. As revealed through the prophet of this dispensation, God "is a discerner of the thoughts and intents of the heart" (D&C 33:1). If a person refrains from a particular act because he is genuinely unable to perform it, but truly would if he could, our Heavenly Father will know this and will reward that person accordingly.[153]

---

153. Oaks, "The Desires of Our Hearts," 66.

Examples of this principle are many, including a person with dietary (or medical) restrictions who cannot fast. Or missionary service that is denied an individual (or modified) due to an impediment like health, worthiness, medications, age, or disabilities. There may be those who desire to give generously to charities, but their financial situation is prohibitive.

"And again, I say unto the poor, ye who have not and yet have sufficient, that ye remain from day to day; I mean all you who deny the beggar, because ye have not; I would that ye say in your hearts that: I give not because I have not, but if I had I would give. And now, if ye say this in your hearts ye remain guiltless" (Mosiah 4:24–25).

Even the lack of attainment of celestial marriage could conceivably come into play. President Lorenzo Snow said,

> There is no Latter-day Saint who dies after having lived a faithful life who will lose anything because of having failed to do certain things when opportunities were not furnished him or her. In other words, if a young man or a young woman has no opportunity of getting married, and they live faithful lives up to the time of their death, they will have all the blessings, exaltation, and glory that any man or woman will have who had this opportunity and improved it. That is sure and positive.[154]

President Packer adds another powerful witness:

> Those who do not marry or those who cannot have children are not excluded from the eternal blessings they seek but which, for now, remain beyond their reach. We do not always know how or when blessings will present themselves, but the promise of eternal increase will not be denied any faithful individual who makes and keeps sacred covenants. Your secret yearnings and tearful pleadings will touch the heart of both the Father and the Son. You will be given a personal assurance from Them that your life will be full and that no blessing that is essential will be lost to you. As a servant of the Lord, acting in the office to which I have been ordained, I give those in such circumstances a promise that there will be nothing essential to your salvation and exaltation that shall not in due time rest upon you. Arms now empty will be filled, and hearts now hurting from broken dreams and yearning will be healed.[155]

154. *The Teachings of Lorenzo Snow,* compiled by Clyde J. Williams (Salt Lake City: Bookcraft, 1984), 138; see also Howard W. Hunter, "Exceeding Great and Precious Promises," *Ensign,* October 1994.

155. Boyd K. Packer, "The Witness," *Ensign,* May 2014.

Restoration and the Atonement

Care must be taken when we discuss the law of restoration. The underlying theme of justice inherent in this law could cloud a true perspective and proper understanding of the doctrine of the Atonement of Jesus Christ.

President Boyd K. Packer perceptively warned, "[The Atonement] is the very root of Christian doctrine. You may know much about the gospel as it branches out from there, but if you only know the branches and those branches do not touch that root, if they have been cut free from that truth, there will be no life nor substance nor redemption in them."[156]

This concept was not lost on Alma as he counseled his son about the meaning of restoration. He succinctly and appropriately ties the Atonement to the doctrine of restoration: "And so it is on the other hand. *If he hath repented of his sins*, and desired righteousness until the end of his days, even so he shall be rewarded unto righteousness . . . *These are they that are redeemed of the Lord . . .* the *way is prepared* that *whosoever will may walk therein and be saved*" (Alma 41:6–8).

Alma was always careful in this regard: giving sinners hope in Christ while assuring a pedagogical balance that would preclude them taking license to sin. He teaches that mercy cannot rob justice (Alma 42:25), but mercy can and does overpower justice! (Alma 34:15). Alma understood that we cannot understate the power and ability of Christ's Atonement to change, redeem, and bless. We must not be either afraid or ashamed to speak of mercy, forgiveness, grace, and God's divine love. However, Christ's abundance of grace and love must always be taught in the context of God's justice. Such is the theme of the continuation of Alma's discourse to Corianton in the next chapter, Alma 42.

C. S. Lewis's words are memorable:

> The Humanitarian theory wants simply to abolish Justice and substitute Mercy for it. Mercy, detached from Justice, grows unmerciful. That is the important paradox. As there are plants which flourish only in mountain soil, so it appears that Mercy will flower only when it grows in the crannies of the rock of Justice: transplanted to the marshlands of mere Humanitarianism, it becomes a man-eating

---

156. Boyd K. Packer, "The Mediator," *Ensign*, May 1977, 56.

weed, all the more dangerous because it is still called by the same name as the mountain variety.[157]

Agency and Restoration

We often hear people say things like, "You are free to make your choice, but not free to choose the consequences of your choices." While basically true, this could be interpreted as meaning that our choices are all our doing, but the consequences are not. This thinking is flawed and could lead to an incorrect understanding of God. We learn from Alma's law of restoration that we not only make the choices, but we willfully choose the consequences as well. Alma is clear about the relationship between actions and outcomes: "Therefore, O my son, whosoever will come may come and partake of the waters of life freely; and whosoever will not come the same is not compelled to come; but in the last day it shall be restored unto him according to his deeds" (Alma 42:27).

This willful choosing of ultimate consequences is similar to Nephi's teaching: "Wherefore, men are free according to the flesh; and all things are given them which are expedient unto man. And they are *free to choose liberty and eternal life, through the great Mediator of all men, or to choose captivity and death*, according to the captivity and power of the devil; for he seeketh that all men might be miserable like unto himself" (2 Nephi 2:27; emphasis added).

Could it be that the prophet Samuel was influenced by the words and idea of Nephi and Alma? Note the similarity and consistency in his teachings in regard to willful choice of ultimate consequences:

And now remember, remember, my brethren, that *whosoever perisheth, perisheth unto himself*; and whosoever doeth iniquity, doeth it unto himself; for behold, *ye are free; ye are permitted to act for yourselves*; for behold, God hath given unto you a knowledge and he hath made you free. He hath given unto you that ye might know good from evil, and he hath given unto you *that ye might choose life or death*; and *ye can do good and be restored unto that which is good, or have that which is good restored unto you; or ye can do evil, and have that which is evil restored unto you.* (Helaman 14:30–31; emphasis added)

---

157. C. S. Lewis, *God in the Dock* (Grand Rapids, MI: Eerdmans, 2014), 294.

One thoughtful observer has noted, "The idea of karma originated in Indian religions such as Hinduism and Buddhism, but is also used in the West to mean that good deeds will be rewarded with good results, with the opposite for bad deeds. . . . The idea of karma is different from the view that what happens is the result of fate, destiny, or what is 'meant to be.' Karma allows room for free will: You make a choice and then benefit or suffer as the result of your choice. In contrast, fate and destiny do not allow room for free will."[158]

Perhaps this what Alma is driving at when he concludes, "And *thus they stand or fall; for behold, they are their own judges,* whether to do good or do evil" (Alma 41:7; emphasis added). In essence, he is trying to teach Corianton that his salvation isn't a function of Nehor's false doctrinal teaching that "all mankind should be saved at the last day, and that they need not fear nor tremble, but that they might lift up their heads and rejoice; for the Lord had created all men, and had also redeemed all men; and, in the end, all men should have eternal life" (Alma 1:4). True, we do not save ourselves, but we do, worlds without end, choose in the first instance to allow Christ to save us!

Law of Restoration and the Natural Man

Another unique and valuable principle that comes from Alma's teaching on restoration has to do with the doctrine of the natural man. To appreciate Alma's doctrinal clarification and scriptural contribution, a little context might be helpful. There are scriptures from the Book of Mormon that are often cited (usually with no context) by well-intentioned teachers to make the claim that mankind is inherently sinful, carnal, lustful, and devilish. By "inherently" we mean that this is the way mankind is natural.

An example often referenced is this verse from the Book of Ether: "O Lord . . . we know that thou art holy and dwellest in the heavens, and that we are unworthy before thee; *because of the fall our natures have become evil continually*" (Ether 3:2; emphasis added). On the surface, this verse seems to imply that because of the fall of Adam and Eve we all are naturally or inherently evil.

---

158. See Paul Thagard's "Karma—What Goes Around Comes Around?," psychologytoday.com; accessed August 5, 2019.

Another verse, part of Alma's counsel to Corianton, has a similar feel: "Therefore, as the soul could never die, and the fall had brought upon all mankind a spiritual death as well as a temporal, that is, they were cut off from the presence of the Lord, it was expedient that mankind should be reclaimed from this spiritual death. Therefore, *as they had become carnal, sensual, and devilish, by nature,* this probationary state became a state for them to prepare; it became a preparatory state" (Alma 42:9–10; emphasis added).

The words "carnal, sensual, and devilish" really seem to sell the *total depravity* doctrine here. But there is another phrase that is even more convincing: "by nature." Both these verses combined make for a strong argument.

However, let us look at some wise counsel from President Boyd K. Packer on the matter of determining doctrine from the scriptures: "Instruction vital to our salvation is not hidden in an obscure verse or phrase in the scriptures," he said. "To the contrary, essential truths are repeated over and over again. Every verse, whether oft-quoted or obscure, must be measured against other verses. There are complementary and tempering teachings in the scriptures which bring a balanced knowledge of truth."[159]

Before considering Alma's teachings on restoration and their connection to the natural man doctrine, let us do as President Packer counsels and examine a few more relevant verses. In the Doctrine and Covenants we find this interesting and helpful verse: "But *by the transgression of these holy laws man became sensual and devilish,* and became fallen man" (D&C 20:20; emphasis added). Let us assume for a moment that mankind is inherently good in the first instance. This verse can help see that perhaps we are not "inherently" evil. However, when we transgress God's "holy laws" our nature can and does change! We *become* sensual and devilish— but we are not necessarily *born* that way. We do not have certain effects of the fall that are entailed on us, however, such as physical or even psychological challenges.

Also helpful are these verses from the Book of Moses: "And Adam and Eve blessed the name of God, and they made all things known unto their sons and their daughters. And Satan came among them, saying: I am also a son of God; and he commanded them, saying: Believe it not [perhaps referring to the teachings of their parents]; and they believed it

---

159. Boyd K. Packer, "The Pattern of Our Parentage," *Ensign*, Nov. 1984, 66.

not, *and they loved Satan more than God.* And *men began from that time forth to be carnal, sensual, and devilish*" (Moses 5:12–13; emphasis added).

Again, assuming we are born inherently good, we once more see in this verse the truth that when we love Satan more than God, and we break the commandments, we become "carnal, sensual, and devilish." We do not, however, start out that way. Other verses from the Book of Mormon also lead to the same conclusion (Mosiah 16:3–5 and Helaman 13:38).

Mosiah 3:19 is a well-known verse and is often used to make the *total depravity* claim. However, when viewed closely, and in light of these other scriptures, another powerful and consistent perspective emerges. In Mosiah we read, "For the natural man is an enemy to God, and has been from the fall of Adam, and will be, forever and ever, unless he yields to the enticings of the Holy Spirit, and *putteth off the natural man* and becometh a saint through the atonement of Christ the Lord, and *becometh as a child*, submissive, meek, humble, patient, full of love, willing to submit to all things which the Lord seeth fit to inflict upon him, even as a child doth submit to his father" (Mosiah 3:19; emphasis added). One might focus here on some of the depravity phrases, like "natural man" (we will explain this further in a moment), and "enemy to God . . . from the fall of Adam." However, we must also consider the phrase "putteth of the natural man," perhaps implying that, like an article of clothing that was once "put on," we likewise, through sin and willful rebellion, at one point "put on" the natural man, whereas, repentance through Christ can allow us to "put off" the natural man. Also, the phrase "become as a child" is important, perhaps suggesting that if we, through sin and disobedience, have come to have a carnal nature, we can, if we choose, use the Atonement to become as a child—not childish, but childlike. This is to say we can use the Atonement of Christ to get back to how we once were, in the first instance, as little children.

Now let's consider these powerful verses from Alma 41 and the law of restoration as President Packer counseled. "And now, my son, all men that are in a *state of nature, or I would say, in a carnal state*, are in the gall of bitterness and in the bonds of iniquity; they are without God in the world, and *they have gone contrary to the nature of God*; therefore, they are in a state contrary to the nature of happiness. And now behold, is the meaning of the word restoration to take a thing of a natural state and place it in an unnatural state, or to place it in a state opposite to its nature?" (Alma 41:11–12; emphasis added).

These verses are interesting and powerful. They are beneficial, in one sense, in helping us understand the phrase "natural man" in Mosiah 3:19. Perhaps this phrase, in light of Alma 41, does not mean this is "natural" the way we are, but rather the natural man, who is in a "state of nature," is in a "carnal state." Thus, the natural man is one who has become carnal through sin and disobedience. Also, if we, through sin, have "gone contrary to the nature of God," this seems to imply what we have been saying, that we did not start out that way. We are inherently good in the first instance, but through the misuse of agency, our nature can change. In summary, President Packer has taught,

> In many churches of the world a doctrine is taught that holds that men are basically evil; that they are earthly and carnal and devilish, conceived in sin and possessed of a tendency to be wicked. This doctrine holds that the corrupt and evil nature of man must be conquered. It holds out the meager hope that by an extension of grace man may, on occasion, be lifted from his evil, carnal, and groveling state. In simple terms, it avers that man is, by his very nature, inclined to be bad. That is false doctrine. I could not accept it to be true and still be a successful teacher. The doctrine is not only false; it is also very destructive. How glorious it is to have the revealed word of God, to know that we have a child-parent relationship with Him. If we are of His family, we have inherited the tendency to be good, not evil. We are sons and daughters of God. It is essential to understand that people are basically good. It is essential to know that their tendency is to do the thing that is right. Such an exalted thought is productive of faith. I am fully aware that in the world there are individuals whose basic motivation seems to be contrary and disruptive and evil. I know this exists, but it is against their nature. If we are to teach, we must constantly remind ourselves that we are dealing with the sons and daughters of God and that each, being His offspring, has the possibility of becoming as He is. I am aware of those scriptural verses that speak of the fallen state of man. I know that some verses describe man's depravity. However, when we take the revelations as a whole, that idea is balanced.[160]

Preparatory Experiences and the Law of Restoration

Alma expands on the law of restoration in the next chapter as he continues to counsel his son Corianton, referring to this life as "*a probationary*

---

160. Boyd K. Packer, *Teach Ye Diligently* (Salt Lake City: Deseret Book, 2004), 88.

time, a time to repent and serve God" (Alma 42:4, emphasis added). This mirrors his earlier teaching in the city of Ammoniah: "There was a space granted unto man in which he might repent; therefore *this life* became *a probationary state; a time to prepare* to meet God; *a time to prepare* for that *endless state which has been spoken of by us, which is after the resurrection of the dead*" (Alma 12:24; emphasis added).

Several important concepts are worth noting in this verse as they pertain to the law of restoration. First, it might be helpful to define what Alma means by his use of the terms, "this life" and "endless state" in Alma 12:24. I would argue that the term "this life" entails more than just "mortal life" but likewise includes our time in the post-mortal spirit world, which is here on this earth and is part of what we could call our *earthly probation* ("probationary time" or "probationary state"). Notice that the text states clearly that the "endless state" comes "after the resurrection of the dead."

Therefore, we find several keys that can help us more correctly interpret another of Alma's associated teachings in Alma 34:32–34:

> For behold, *this life* [earthly probation, including the post-spirit world] is the time for men *to prepare to meet God* [in heaven]; yea, behold the *day of this life* [earthly probation] is the day for men to perform their labors [note that we can still perform these labors, or, have them preformed for us vicariously while in the post-mortal spirit world]. And now, as I said unto you before, as ye have had so many witnesses, therefore, I beseech of you that ye do not procrastinate the *day of your repentance* [here in our early probation . . . and yes, one can repent in the spirit world and receive baptism] until the end [not the end of this mortal life, but the end, meaning resurrection and judgment]; for *after this day of life*, which is *given us to prepare for eternity* [not the post-mortal spirit world], behold, if we do not improve our time while *in this life* [earthly probation], then cometh the *night of darkness* [resurrection and judgment, not mortal death] wherein there can be *no labor performed* [again, we can perform labors in the post-mortal spirit world]. Ye cannot say, when ye are brought to *that awful crisis* [not mortal death, but resurrection and judgment], that I will repent, that I will return to my God. Nay, ye cannot say this; for that same spirit which doth possess your bodies at the time that ye go out of *this life* [earthly probation], that same spirit will have power to

possess your body in that *eternal world* [not spirit world]. (Alma 34:32–34; emphasis added)[161]

Case in point, if our "spirit" is possessing our "body" in that "eternal world," it could not be the spirit world (since we do not have physical bodies there) but would have to be that resurrected state (eternal world) when our "spirit and the body shall be reunited again in its perfect form; both limb and joint shall be restored to its proper frame, even as we now are at this time" (Alma 11:43–44). The following diagram might be helpful in visualizing the terms being discussed herein. Elder Neal A. Maxwell referred to the plan of salvation as a "three-act" play.[162] I would argue that each act could be divided into two scenes each:

Pre-Earth Life		Earthly Probation		Eternity	
I	II	III	IV	V	VI
Intelligence	Spirit	Mortal Probation	Spirit World	Resurrection	Godhood / Perfection

---

161. An excellent article on the potential meanings of the specific words and phrases in these verses can be found in Larry E. Dahl's "The Concept of Hell," 1991 Sperry Symposium at BYU, 42–56. Although Brother Dahl's interpretation of some specific words is different than those purposed in this book, the general conclusions that both reach are the same.

162. Neal A. Maxwell, "Enduring Well," *Ensign*, Apr. 1997, 7. Also note the following statement from the first presidency (Smith, Winder, and Lund, "The Origin of Man," 1909) in reference to the potential difference between scenes five and six on the diagram: "Man is the child of God, formed in the divine image and endowed with divine attributes, and even as the infant son of an earthly father and mother is capable in due time of becoming a man, so the undeveloped offspring of celestial parentage is capable, by experience through ages and eons, of evolving into a God." See also the Feb. 2002 *Ensign*.

Second, this life is not only a "probationary state" or "time,"[163] but likewise a time to "prepare" for our next estate (third estate), or "eternity" as Alma would say (Alma 34:34), or "endless state" (Alma 12:24). This is to say that the law of restoration is more than just a law of causality, reaping what we sow. It has a purpose in preparing one's soul for this third act in the plan of salvation. Perhaps this preparatory aspect of the law of restoration is what Alma is referring to when he states, "Therefore, *all things shall be restored* to their *proper order*, every thing to its *natural frame*—mortality raised to immortality, corruption to incorruption—raised to endless happiness to inherit the kingdom of God, or to endless misery to inherit the kingdom of the devil, the one on one hand, the other on the other" (Alma 41:4). In other words, not just resurrected bodies, but rather "all things."

Often, a question is raised that goes something like this: "What will we be doing in Heaven?" While we might not know all the divine specifics of our eternal future, we can surmise some general realities based upon Alma's law of restoration, especially as it applies to preparatory aspect.

Service and Ministering as Preparation

President Marion G. Romney wisely counseled, "Service is not something we endure on this earth so we can earn the right to live in the celestial kingdom. Service is the very fiber of which an exalted life in the celestial kingdom is made."[164] In other words, if we do not like serving while here in our earthly probation, we probably will not enjoy the celestial kingdom!

Sister Jean B. Bingham has similarly stated,

What a wonderful blessing to live in a time of continual revelation from God! As we look forward to and embrace the "restitution of all things," which has and will come through the prophesied events of our time, *we are being prepared for the Savior's Second Coming.* And *what better way to prepare* to meet Him than to strive to become like Him *through lovingly ministering to one another!*[165]

---

163. Probationary in this sense can denote a time of trial or a time of testing.

164. Romney, "The Celestial Nature of Self-Reliance," 93.

165. Jean B. Bingham, "Ministering as the Savior Does," *Ensign*, May 2018; emphasis added.

Missionary Work as Preparation

Elder Neal A. Maxwell said, "What we do here is so vital but is actually *a preparation for our labors in paradise in the spirit world.* The scope in that spirit world is ten times as large as are the demographics of this world. It is, though, a place of peace, a place of intense devotion."[166] Likewise, in the Doctrine and Covenants we learn, "I beheld that the faithful elders of this dispensation, when they depart from mortal life, *continue their labors in the preaching of the gospel of repentance and redemption,* through the sacrifice of the Only Begotten Son of God, among those who are in darkness and under the bondage of sin in the great world of the spirits of the dead" (D&C 138:57; emphasis added).

Knowledge as Preparation

Joseph Fielding Smith has stated, "It is not because the Lord is ignorant of law and truth that he is able to progress, *but because of his knowledge and wisdom.* The Lord is constantly using his knowledge in his work. And his great work is in bringing to pass the immortality and eternal life of man. By the creation of worlds and peopling them, by building and extending, he progresses, but not because the fulness of truth is not understood by him."[167] In other words, "Whatever principle of intelligence we attain unto in this life, *it will rise with us in the resurrection.* And if a person gains more knowledge and intelligence in this life through his diligence and obedience than another, *he will have so much the advantage in the world to come*" (D&C 130:18–19).

Family as Preparation

It could be said that the comparatively small family units that we live in can also be a preparation for the family unit in the next estate, though at a much greater scale. In The Family: A Proclamation to the World," we read, "The divine plan of happiness *enables family relationships to be perpetuated beyond the grave.* Sacred ordinances and covenants available

---

166. Neal A. Maxwell, CES Fireside, 2 Feb. 2001.

167. Smith, *Doctrines of Salvation*, 1:10.29.

in holy temples make it possible for individuals to return to the presence of God and for families to be united eternally."[168]

Consecration as Preparation

The scriptures tell us that "you may be equal in the bonds of heavenly things, yea, and earthly things also, for the obtaining of heavenly things. For *if ye are not equal in earthly things ye cannot be equal in obtaining heavenly things*; For if you will that I give unto you a place in the celestial world, *you must prepare yourselves* by doing the things which I have commanded you and required of you" (D&C 78:5–7; emphasis added).

Trials and Suffering as Preparation

Even the trials and sufferings of this life can serve as a preparation for the type of divine suffering we will surely endure eternally as exalted beings. To be clear, this type of suffering should not be confused with the suffering of the wicked (see D&C 19:15–19; 76:44–49; Mormon 2:13). For example, in Moses 7 we learn that "the God of heaven looked upon the residue of the people, *and he wept*; and Enoch bore record of it, saying: *How is it that the heavens weep*, and shed forth their tears as the rain upon the mountains? And Enoch said unto the Lord: *How is it that thou canst weep*, seeing thou art holy, and from all eternity to all eternity? (Moses 7:28–29: emphasis added). This is to say, that exalted beings can and do experience sadness, perhaps to degrees we do not fully comprehend, for the sinful mistakes of their spirit children." (See also 3 Nephi 28:9.)

Terryl L. Givens observed, "God is not exempt from emotional pain . . . On the contrary, God's pain is as infinite as His love."[169]

Perhaps the admonition in Mosiah 18 to "mourn with those that mourn" is not only a required aspect of discipleship in this life, but also a preparation for the eternities. We are not just trying to get "suffering" done with. No. It too is a preparation. Elder Neal A. Maxwell observed, "Rather than simply passing through trials, we must allow trials to pass through us in ways that sanctify us."[170] It could be said, in light of these

---

168. "The Family: A Proclamation to the World"; emphasis added.
169. Terryl L. and Fiona Givens, *The God Who Weeps: How Mormonism Makes Sense of Life* (Salt Lake City: Ensign Peak, 2012).
170. Maxwell, "Enduring Well."

daunting truths, that eternal life and heaven are not an absence of pain, but rather a fulness of joy. And Heavenly Father's desire and plan is to prepare us accordingly.

Conclusion

As Alma completes his discussion of the law of restoration, he gives four examples of things we ought to do: "Therefore, my son, *see that you are merciful* unto your brethren; *deal justly, judge righteously,* and *do good continually*; and if ye do all these things then shall ye receive your reward; yea, ye shall have mercy restored unto you again; ye shall have justice restored unto you again; ye shall have a righteous judgment restored unto you again; and ye shall have good rewarded unto you again. For that which ye do send out shall return unto you again, and be restored; therefore, the word restoration more fully condemneth the sinner, and justifieth him not at all" (Alma 41:14–15; emphasis added).

Alma's law of restoration is a vital doctrine in the restored gospel of Jesus Christ. It is a powerful concept that ties us to God the Father and his son, Jesus Christ. It embraces and frames the purpose and intent of the very plan of salvation itself. It demands we walk the path of justice, while ensuring that the mercies of the Atonement can empower us to take the proper steps. It invites us to treat others with kindness, respect, and charity. It lifts us from idleness and mediocrity, allowing us to become what we were eternally designed to be. It urges us to use our agency wisely: inviting us not only to consider our choices in life but also to take direct responsibility for the outcomes of those choices. It teaches us why what we do here in this earth life matters, and how our choices serve as a small preparation for the glorious realities in the eternities to come. In short, it helps us to exclaim,

> How great, how glorious, how complete
> Redemption's grand design,
> Where justice, love, and mercy meet
> In harmony divine![171]

---

171. "How Great the Wisdom and the Love," *Hymns*, no. 195.

About the Author

C. Robert Line has worked full time with religious education for the past twenty-five years. In addition to teaching with the BYU Religious Education faculty, he has been a presenter at BYU Education Week, Women's Conference, and Especially for Youth and has worked for Church Educational System programs as an instructor and director for Institutes of Religion. Brother Line has both a bachelor's and master's degree from BYU and also holds a doctoral degree from Purdue University in sociology of religion. He has authored various books and articles and has served as the editor in chief of *Century Magazine*. Brother Line has served in the Church as a bishop, stake high councilor, elders quorum president, and various other callings. He played on the BYU men's basketball team from 1984 to 1985. He and his wife, Tamera Wright Line, have five children and six grandchildren. Their family resides in Cedar Hills, Utah.

Scan to visit

www.crobline.com

—